ISBN 978-1-331-30164-6
PIBN 10171296

1 MONTH OF
FREE
READING

at
www.ForgottenBooks.com

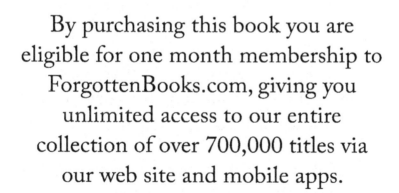

By purchasing this book you are eligible for one month membership to ForgottenBooks.com, giving you unlimited access to our entire collection of over 700,000 titles via our web site and mobile apps.

To claim your free month visit:

www.forgottenbooks.com/free171296

English
Français
Deutsche
Italiano
Español
Português

www.forgottenbooks.com

Mythology Photography **Fiction**
Fishing Christianity **Art** Cooking
Essays Buddhism Freemasonry
Medicine **Biology** Music **Ancient**
Egypt Evolution Carpentry Physics
Dance Geology **Mathematics** Fitness
Shakespeare **Folklore** Yoga Marketing
Confidence Immortality Biographies
Poetry **Psychology** Witchcraft
Electronics Chemistry History **Law**
Accounting **Philosophy** Anthropology
Alchemy Drama Quantum Mechanics
Atheism Sexual Health **Ancient History**
Entrepreneurship Languages Sport
Paleontology Needlework Islam
Metaphysics Investment Archaeology
Parenting Statistics Criminology
Motivational

CLIMBING IN THE BRITISH ISLES

ENGLAND

CLIMBING

IN THE BRITISH ISLES

3 vols. 16mo.   Sold separately.

———

I.   ENGLAND.

II.   WALES.   *[In preparation.*

III.   SCOTLAND.   *[In preparation.*

———

LONDON AND NEW YORK:
LONGMANS, GREEN, AND CO.

CLIMBING

IN

THE BRITISH ISLES

I.—ENGLAND

BY

W. P. HASKETT SMITH, M.A.

MEMBER OF THE ALPINE CLUB

WITH TWENTY-THREE ILLUSTRATIONS
BY
ELLIS CARR
MEMBER OF THE ALPINE CLUB

AND FIVE PLANS

LONDON
LONGMANS, GREEN, AND CO.
AND NEW YORK : 15 EAST 16th STREET
1894

CONTENTS

INTRODUCTION

The headings, for convenience of reference, are arranged in one continuous alphabetical series, comprising the following classes of subject :

INTRODUCTION

FOR some years past there has been a remarkably rapid increase in the number of men who climb for climbing's sake within the bounds of the British Isles.

When any young and active Englishman sees a rock and is told that the ascent of it is regarded as a kind of feat, there is no doubt what he will want to do. He will obey what has been the instinct of the race at any time this forty years. But lately there has been a change. What was formerly done casually and instinctively has for the last dozen years or so been done systematically and of set purpose, for it is now recognised that hill-climbing in these islands may form part of a real mountaineering education. Many might-be mountaineers have missed their vocation because they were in the position of the prudent individual who would not go into the water until after he should have learned to swim : they did not become Alpine because they were afraid that they should make fools of themselves if they went on the Alps. Yet, had they only known it, they might have found without crossing the sea many a place which might have been to their undeveloped instincts what the little pond at the end of the garden has been to many a would-be skater—a quiet spot where early flounderings would be safe from the contemptuous glances of unsympathetic experts.

Icemanship can only be acquired through a long apprenticeship, by tramping many a weary mile helplessly tied to the tail of a guide. But one principal charm of hill-climbing lies in the fact that it may be picked up by self-directed practice and does not demand the same preliminary subjection. The course of Alpine instruction can only be considered complete when Mr. Girdlestone's ideal of 'The High Alps without Guides' is realised (an ideal, be it clearly understood, which for fully ninety-nine out of every hundred climbers it would be downright madness to attempt to carry into practice) ; whereas, while rock-climbing may be enjoyed by amateurs without incurring the reproach of recklessness, they at the same time experience the exquisite pleasure of forming their own plans of attack, of varying the execution of them according to their own judgment, and finally of meeting obstacles, as they arise, with their own skill and with their own strength, and overcoming them without the assistance of a hired professional.

Nowhere can the mere manual dexterity of climbing be better acquired than among the fells of Cumberland; excellent practising-ground presents itself on nearly every hill. Compared with real mountains the crags of Cumberland are but toys, but small as they are, they have made many and many a fine climber; and the man who has gone through a course of training among them, who has learnt to know the exact length of his own stride and reach, and to wriggle up a 'chimney' in approved style with shoulder, hip and knee, may boldly fly at higher game, and when he proceeds to tackle the giants of the Alps or Caucasus has no cause to be afraid of the result.

As if with the express object of increasing their educational value to the mountaineer, the hilly parts of Great Britain are peculiarly subject to atmospheric changes. No one who has not experienced their effects would believe the extent to which mist, snow, and even rain can change the appearance of landmarks among the mountains; and, where landmarks are less abundant or less striking, even the buffeting of violent wind may cause an inexperienced man to change his direction unconsciously. Valuable experience in things of this kind may be gained even in summer, but in winter the conditions become more Alpine, and splendid practice may be had in the use of the axe and rope.

Not that the latter should be neglected on difficult rocks at any time of the year. Even in places where it gives the leader no security and to some extent actually impedes him, the moral effect of it is good. It wonderfully increases those feelings of united and ordered effort, of mutual dependence and mutual confidence, and finally of cheery subordination of self, which are not the least of the virtues or the joys of mountaineering. How these opportunities may be used the novice will readily learn from Mr. Charles Pilkington's admirable chapters in the Badminton 'Mountaineering,' and from Dr. Claude Wilson's excellent little handbook on the same subject. It is the aim of the present work to enable him to find suitable places where the principles so admirably laid down by those authorities may be tested and applied, and to understand the descriptions—often involving difficult technical and local terms—which have been published of them. When anyone with climbing instincts finds himself in a strange place his first desire is to discover a climb, his second to learn what its associations are ; what is it called, and why ? has anyone climbed it, and what did he think of it ? To such questions as these this book endeavours to pro- vide an answer. It offers, in short, to the would-be climber a link, with the guidebook on the one hand and the local specialist on the other.

It must always be remembered that a very fine rock may be a very poor climb. It may be impossible or it may be too easy, or, again, the material may be dangerously rotten ; and thus, though there are many places where men can and do obtain useful climbing practice, there is only one part of England to which resort is made simply for the sake of its climbing. In consequence of this fact the greater part of the book is devoted to the English Lakes, and especially to the south-west portion of them, where the best climbs of all are to be found. But in that district the art has been highly elaborated, and the standard of difficulty and dexterity is even dangerously high. If men would be content to serve an apprenticeship and to feel their way gradually from the easier climbs onward, they would excite less apprehension in the minds of those who know what these climbs are. If, on the other hand, they rush, as too many do, straight from the desk in a crowded city, with unseasoned lungs and muscles, in the cold and the wet, to attack alone or with chance companions whatever climb enjoys for the moment the greatest notoriety, frightful accidents are certain to occur.

The books, too, which are kept specially for climbing records at some places in the Lakes, such as Dungeon Gill, Buttermere, and, notably, Wastdale Head, are misleading, owing to the widely different standards of difficulty among the various writers. Printed accounts are so few that this objection hardly applies to them. The most noteworthy beyond all doubt are the two articles written for *All the Year Round*, in November 1884, by Mr. C. N. Williamson, the late editor of *Black and White*. It would be hard to exaggerate the effect which these articles had in making the Lake climbs known. The same writer had previously contributed articles of less permanent value to the *Graphic* and the *Daily News*. In 1837 two articles had appeared in the *Penny Magazine* (see *Lord's Rake*); in 1859 the late Professor Tyndall had written of *Mickledoor* in the *Saturday Review*, and more recently articles have appeared in the *Pall Mall Gazette*, by Mr. W. Brunskill and by Mr. H. A. Gwynne. The present writer contributed an article to the *Alpine Journal* of August 1892, and one containing very clear illustrations of 'back-and-knee' work and of an episode in the long climb on the Pillar Rock to the pages of *Black and White*, in June 1892, while numerous articles have appeared from time to time in such local papers as the *Whitehaven News* and the *West Cumberland Times*, and in the Manchester, Leeds, and Bradford press. Of guidebooks the only one of any value to climbers is Mr. Herman Prior's ' Pedestrian Guide.'

Any value which the present book may have is largely due to the excellent drawings of Mr. Ellis Carr, who most kindly came forward to fill the place left by the lamented death of Professor A. M. Marshall. Much assistance has been derived from sketches and photographs kindly lent, those of Mr. Abraham, of Keswick, being especially useful. For the valuable article on ' Chalk ' I am indebted to Mr. A. F. Mummery, whose knowledge of the subject is unrivalled ; while Mr. J. W. Robinson, of Lorton, has zealously assisted in all matters connected with Cumberland ; and I must gratefully acknowledge help given in other ways by Mr. J. E. Morris and the Rev. C. J. Buckmaster.

CLIMBING

IN

THE BRITISH ISLES

———◦◦◦———

ENGLAND

Alum Pot, the name of which is also found in such forms as *Allen* and *Hellan*, lies just west of the Midland Railway, about halfway between Horton and Ribblehead stations, and on the north-east side of Ingleborough. It is one of the most striking and most famous of the Yorkshire potholes, being an elliptical opening in the limestone, 120 ft. long and 40 ft. wide, with a perpendicular depth of 200 ft. The exploration of it was begun by Mr. Birkbeck of Anley in 1847, who, assisted by Prof. Boyd Dawkins and a large party including three ladies, made a complete examination in 1870.

Angler's Crag, on the south side of Ennerdale Water. The steep portion is about 300 ft. There are also some similar crags on *Grike* and *Revelin*, close by; but none of them are worth a long walk, and the only resting-place near is the Angler's Inn, at the foot of Ennerdale Water.

Apron-strings.—Throughout Scotland and the North of England the traditional explanation of large heaps of stones is that while some one (generally the Devil or Samson) was carrying the stones in his apron the strings broke and the stones fell in a heap. Many such heaps are to be found, bearing the name of 'apronful' or 'bratful,' which means the same thing. A good instance of the latter form is *Samson's Bratful*, in Cumberland, between the rivers Bleng and Calder. For another good instance see what is said about Wade's Causeway in *Murray's Handbook for Yorkshire*, at p. 206.

Aron.—So Wilkinson (in his 'Select Views') calls *Great End*. It may be that he misunderstood his guide, who was, perhaps, speaking at the time of *Aaron Crags*, which are on *Sprinkling Fell*, and would be in the line of sight to any one coming up from *Borrowdale*. In fact, the path to *Sty Head* passes not only *Aaron Crags* on the left, but also *Aaron Slack* on the right. It is, of course, tempting to suggest that Aron was the original Keltic name of Great End; but in Wales the name Aran is generally applied to mountains of very different appearance to *Great End*.

Arrowhead, a prominent rock in the *Napes* of *Great Gable*, being part of the ridge immediately west of *Eagle's Nest*. It was climbed on April 17, 1892, by a large party, including Messrs. Horace Walker, Baker, Slingsby, and others. In the following year, on the last day of March, this climb was repeated by Messrs. Solly, Schintz, Brant, and Bowen, who continued it right on to the top of the ridge. They kept rather more on the ridge itself than the former party had done on the way to the *Arrowhead,* and from that point

THE ARROWHEAD
(South side of Great Gable)

the climb is along the crest of the ridge. It is not a difficult climb for an experienced party. The ridge has been called the *Arrowhead Ridge.*

Ash Crag, a rock in *Ennerdale,* near the *Black Sail* end of the *Pillar Fell.* It is the writer's belief that this is the rock which the poet Wordsworth, in ' The Brothers,' has confused with the *Pillar Rock.* At least a lad belonging to an old Ennerdale family, the Bowmans of Mireside, was killed by falling from this rock at a date closely corresponding to that indicated in the poem.

Attermire, one of the most picturesque limestone scars in Yorkshire. It is reached from Settle on the Midland Railway, and may be seen on the way to Malham Cove.

Back-and-knee : the process of supporting or raising the body in a ' chimney ' by pressure against opposite sides with back and knees, or, more usually, back and feet.

Band.—This word forms part of many hill names in the North of England, and is also found in Scotland. Dr. Murray deals with it in the ' New English Dictionary,' but not in a satisfactory manner. He defines it as ' a long ridge-like hill of minor height or a long narrow sloping offshoot from a hill or mountain,' but it would be easy to adduce instances where this could have no application. The word is used by Douglas in his translation of Virgil to represent the Latin word ' jugum ' :

Himself ascendis the hie *band* of the hill ;

and from this Jamieson concluded that the word meant simply ' top of a hill '—a definition almost as unsuitable as the last. The late Mr. Dickinson, the leading authority on the Cumberland dialect, gave to the word the meaning of 'a boundary on high uninclosed land,' and indeed the frequent association of the word with personal names (often of clearly Scandinavian character) seems to indicate some territorial significance.

Bannerdale Crag (C. sh. 57) may be taken on the way up *Saddleback* from Troutbeck station on the line between Keswick and Penrith. About three miles up the stream is *Mungrisdale*, and still farther up along the course of the stream one fork leads to *Scales Tarn* and another to *Bannerdale*, where there is a lead mine just north of the crags. There is a rocky face some 600 ft. to 800 ft. high, offering climbing, which is steep, but by no means first-rate.

Barf.—From the southern shore of Bassenthwaite Water there is a fine steep scramble up this hill. On a bright winter's day it is rather inspiriting, and the views are good.

The name is more frequent in Yorkshire, where, according to Phillips, it has the meaning of 'a detached low ridge or hill.'

Beachy Head, close to Eastbourne, in Sussex, is a very fine bold chalk cliff, the first ascent of which is made about once in every two years, if we may believe all that we see in the papers. The truth is that there is a treacherous incline of some 600 ft., formed of chalk and grass, both very steep and often dangerously slippery; and during the Eastbourne season the coastguards at the top find their principal occupation in supplying mechanical assistance to exhausted clamberers; but for difficulty these cliffs will not for a moment compare with those of half the height which carry on the line westward to *Birling Gap*. The tops of these in many places literally overhang the sea, and there are few points where a climber could make the slightest impression upon them. On Beachy Head there is a dangerous-looking pinnacle, which was climbed (by dint of cutting a step or two) in April 1894, by Mr. E. A. Crowley.

Bear Rock, a queerly-shaped rock on *Great Napes*, which in the middle of March 1889 was gravely attacked by a large party comprising some five or six of the strongest climbers in England. It is a little difficult to find, especially in seasons when the grass is at all long.

Beck.—In the North of England (except in Northumberland and Durham, where 'burn' prevails) this is the usual word for a brook. It differs from a 'gill' in being more open, and having banks less rocky and a stream somewhat more copious. A gill may contain only a few drops of water, or none at all, and still preserve its self-respect, but not so a beck. Camden speaks of 'Beakes and Brookes.'

Bell enters into many North Country hill-names. It is commonly said to indicate spots which were specially devoted to the worship of Baal, and many arguments have been based upon its occurrence and distribution. If there is anything in this assertion, the 'high places' for the worship of Baal must have been most capriciously selected. My own belief is that the term is purely descriptive and is applied to a convexity in the slope of a hill. In Lowland Scotch the phrase 'bell of the brae' is not uncommon and has the same significance.

Bell Rib End, a short drop on the narrow south ridge of *Yewbarrow.* Though on a very small scale, it is not without interest, and was a favourite with Mr. Maitland, one of the early explorers of Wastdale.

Bield.—This word not only occurs frequently in place names, but is still part of living speech in North England and South Scotland. It means shelter of any kind for man or beast, and in the latter case especially a fox or a sheep. It is also used as a verb ; in fox hunting, for instance, the animal when run to earth is said to be ' bielded.'

Bink: a long narrow grassy ledge. (N. of Eng.)

Black Sail.—It has been suggested that this name, now borne by the pass from Wastdale to Ennerdale between Pillarfell and Kirkfell, may have originally been named from the mountain it crossed, and so may possibly now preserve an older name of one of those two mountains. Dr. Murray, writing to a local paper some years ago, did not hesitate to affirm positively that Pillar Fell is entirely due to the Ordnance surveyors, and that the original name was Black Sail, a fact which he said could be proved by historical evidence. It would be extremely interesting to see this evidence, but the name ' Pillar ' certainly appears in maps published long before that of the Ordnance. (See *Sail.*) The pass (1,750 ft.) is very familiar to all climbing folk, being the ordinary way of reaching the Pillar Rock from Wastdale Head. It is generally preferred to *Wind Gap* on account of greater

variety of view and better 'going,' and some make use of it
even for the purpose of reaching the Ennerdale side of *Great
Gable.*

The route, however, has one disadvantage. It is hot. It
is no uncommon thing to hear enthusiastic frequenters of the
Lakes complaining of the popular misapprehension that the
sun never shines there, and urging that people are so unreason-
able as to notice the wet but to disregard the warmth.
Among these traducers of the Cumberland climate the frequenters of the Black Sail route are not found. Argue not
with such ; but some fair morning, when the reviler is most
rampant, lead him gently into Mosedale and watch with calm
delight while he pants painfully up the pass, trying his
utmost to look cool, with the sun, which he has maligned,
beating down squarely upon his back and exacting a merciless
revenge. Many a time will he turn about and feign rapture
at the taper cone of Yewbarrow and the bold outline of
Scafell ; often will his bootlace strangely come untied before
his reverted glance catches the welcome gleam of Burnmoor
Tarn ; but long before that time his heart within him will
have melted even as wax, and he will have registered a vow
that, when next the Cumberland sunshine is discussed, the
seat of the scornful shall know him no more. Mr. James Payn,
having occasion to allude to 'dry weather' in the Lakes, adds
demurely, 'which is said to have occurred about the year
1824 '; but, from his own description of Black Sail, it is clear
that he deeply rued the sarcasm : 'You will begin to find
your pass quite sufficiently steep. Indeed, this is the severest
pull of any of the cols in the District, and has proved the

friend of many a gallant with his ladylove. To offer a young woman your hand when you are going up Black Sail is in my mind one of the greatest proofs of attachment that can be given, and, if she accepts it, it is tantamount to the everlasting " Yes ! " ' We may be sure that, before he reached the top, the witty novelist experienced remarkably ' dry weather,' and also some of those symptoms which elsewhere he has himself described with such scientific accuracy : ' Inordinate perspiration and a desperate desire for liquids; if the ascent be persisted in, the speech becomes affected to the extent of a total suspension of conversation. The temper then breaks down ; an unseemly craving to leave our companion behind, and a fiendish resolution not to wait for him if his bootlace comes undone, distinguish the next stage of the climbing fever ; all admiration of the picturesque has long since vanished, exuded, I fancy, through the pores of the skin : nothing remains but Selfishness, Fatigue, and the hideous reflection that the higher we go the longer will be our journey down again. The notion of malignant spirits occupying elevated regions — Fiends of the Fell—doubtless arose from the immoral experiences of the Early Climbers.'

Green's *Guide* (1819) records a touching instance of a husband's attentions surviving a test which we saw above, that even lovers find severe : ' This is a steep and craggy ascent, and so laborious to man that it might be imagined horses could not travel it; yet Mr. Thomas Tyson, of Wasdale Head, has conducted Mrs. Tyson over this stony ground while sitting on the back of her horse.'

In Switzerland one might look back after a day's work,

and fairly forget ups and downs so slight as Black Sail; but many of the guide books speak of it in terms which might apply to the Adler or the Felik Joch. For instance, *Black's Picturesque Guide* (ed. 1872) says: 'The *hardy* pedestrian with *very minute* instructions *might* succeed in finding his way over the mountains, yet every one who has crossed them will beware of the danger of the attempt and of the *occasional fatal consequences* attending a diversion from the proper path.' This is highly encouraging; and the enterprising traveller who only breaks his neck two or three times in the course of the journey will be of good cheer, for he is making rather a prosperous expedition than otherwise.

Blea Crag, an isolated square stone on the left of the path to the *Stake*, a long mile up *Longstrath*. It is climbed on the side which looks down the valley. Messrs. Jones and Robinson recorded their ascent of it in September 1893, but it seems that four or five years ago there were traces on it of a previous ascent.

'Crag' is not very commonly used of a single stone, as it is here and in the case of *Carl Crag*.

Borrowdale.—'Divers Springes,' says old Leland in his 'Itinerary,' 'cummeth owt of Borodale, and so make a great *Lowgh that we cawle a Poole.*'

The 'Lowgh' is, of course, Derwentwater, and Borrowdale is the heart of the finest scenery and the best climbing in England. It may be said to stretch from *Scafell* to *Skiddaw*, and excellent headquarters for climbers may be found in it at *Lowdore*, *Grange*, *Rosthwaite*, and *Seatoller*. With the aid of its wad mines and its *Bowder Stone*, it probably did more during last century than anything else to arouse public interest in the Lake country. The natives were not famed for their intelligence, and many stories are told in support of their nickname of ' Borrowdale gowks.'

There is another *Borrowdale* in Westmorland, and *Boredale* is perhaps the same name.

Bowder Stone in *Borrowdale* was already a curiosity about a century and a half ago, when it was visited by Mr. George Smith, the correspondent of the *Gentleman's Magazine*. Clarke, writing some years later, says it bore the alternative names of *Powderstone* and *Bounderstone*, and being ' thirty-one yards long by eight yards high, must therefore weigh over 600 tons, and is said to be the largest self-stone in England.' It is not really a ' boulder ' at all, but the word is rather loosely used in Cumberland.

Bow Fell (2,960 ft.).—The name is probably the same as that of *Baugh Fell*, also called *Bow Fell*, in Yorkshire. This graceful peak, standing as it does at the head of several important valleys—*Eskdale, Langdale, Dunnerdale*, and *Borrowdale*—is a great feature in Lake scenery. There is not much rock-work on it, but a good deal of rough walking and scrambling. From *Borrowdale* or *Wastdale* it is approached by way of *Esk Hause*. On this side there is no climbing, except that *Hanging Knot*, as the N. end of Bow Fell is called, descends to *Angle Tarn* in a long, steep, rocky slope which offers a pleasant scramble.

On the *Eskdale* side there is a gully or two which might be worth exploring.

By inclining to the right hand on emerging at the top of *Hell Gill*, or to the left hand from the pony-track at the foot of *Rossett Gill* we reach *Flat Crags*, huge glacier-planed slopes of rock, overlooked by what in winter is a fine *couloir* of most alpine appearance. When Messrs. J. & A. R. Stogdon ascended it (*Alpine Journal*, v. p. 35) the inclination of the snow increased from 30° at the foot to 63° after 350 ft. or more, and there was a large cornice at the top. In the account which the same party inserted at the time in the Wastdale Head Book steeper angles are given.

In summer it is merely an open scree-gully; but the insignificant-looking chimney just N. of it, and only separated from it by a narrow ridge, is quite worthy of attention, though it has but one pitch in it after the one at the foot. The descent is harder than the ascent, and takes about twenty minutes.

There is a fine rocky walk along the S. ridge, called *Shelter Crags* and *Crinkle Crags*, which descends towards the head of Dunnerdale, but it is extremely unfrequented.

Bram Crag and *Wanthwaite Crag* flank the coach road between *Threlkeld* and *Grasmere* on the east. The best part is rather more than two miles south of Threlkeld station. The climbing is somewhat similar to that about *Swarthbeck* on Ullswater, but on better and sounder rock, and there is more of it. A good day's work will be found among these crags, and a fine specimen of a 'sledgate' is deserving of notice.

Brandreth is between *Borrowdale* and the head of *Ennerdale.* The name, which occurs elsewhere in the neighbourhood, denotes a tripod (literally a ' grate,' usually made with three legs). The meeting-point of three boundaries of counties, parishes, &c. is often so named. Brandreth has only one short bit of bold rock—one of the many *Raven Crags.* It is hardly worth a special journey, but may very easily be taken by any one who attacks *Great Gable* from *Borrowdale.*

Brimham Rocks, in Yorkshire, are very easily visited from Harrogate or from Pateley Bridge. From the latter they are only four miles to the eastward. The station for those who come from Harrogate is Dacre Banks, from which the Rocks may be reached in an hour's walking. They are of millstone grit and well deserve a visit, for nowhere are the grotesque forms which that material delights to assume more remarkable. Some resemble the sandstone forms common about Tunbridge Wells, and many might very well stand for Dartmoor Tors ; but others at first sight seem so evidently and unmistakably to suggest human handiwork that one can feel no surprise at the common notion that they were fashioned by the ingenuity of the Druids. Several of them, though very small, can only be climbed with considerable difficulty.

Broad Stand—a term commonly but, in my opinion, incorrectly used to denote a particular route by which the crags of *Scafell* may be ascended direct from *Mickledoor.* There are numerous other places within a few miles of this into the names of which this word 'stand' enters, and a consideration of them leads me to the belief that it signifies 'a large grassy plot of ground awkward of access.' This is exactly what we find here. A break in the cliffs produces a large open space which is the key to the ascent by the *Mickledoor Chimney*, to that by the *North Climb*, and to that which, being the oldest, easiest, and most frequented, has arrogated to itself as distinctive the name of a feature which it should only share with the other two. Really all three routes are merely different ways of reaching the Broad Stand.

One of the earliest recorded ascents is that of Mr. C. A. O. Baumgartner in September 1850, an account of which was sent by one of the people of the dale to the local paper in these terms : 'The Broad Stand, *a rocky and dangerous precipice*, situated between *Scaw Fell* and the *Pikes*, an ascent which is perhaps more difficult than even that of the *Pillar Stone*.' The late Professor Tyndall climbed it in 1859, and described it in the *Saturday Review* of that year. It evidently had a great reputation then, which was not, in his opinion, entirely deserved. It seems to have been known in 1837 (see the *Penny Magazine*) to the shepherds; and even in Green's time, at the beginning of the century, one or two daring spirits had accomplished the feat.

Buckbarrow (C. sh. 79).—*Broadcrag* (more north-east) is really part of it, and about 400 ft. high. Buckbarrow rises near the foot of Wastwater, opposite the best part of the Screes. When approached from the head of the lake it appears as two huge rocky steps; but, as in the case of *Eagle Crag* in *Greenup*, the steps are not really in the same plane. Seen from the slopes of *Lingmell*, it forms the boundary between the mountains and the plain, to which it sinks in one very graceful concave curve. It is not lofty—there are perhaps some 400 ft. of rock—but by the shepherds it is reputed inaccessible. This is only true in the sense that there are stiff bits on it which have to be evaded. It is haunted by both the fox and the buzzard—connoisseurs on whose taste in rocks the climber can generally rely. There is also climbing in the whole line of rock (Broad Crag) which stretches away towards *Greendale*. Since 1884, when the writer first became acquainted with it, Buckbarrow has become rather popular, considering its remoteness from *Wastdale Head.*—At Christmas 1891 a strong party, led by Messrs. Robinson, Hastings, and Collie, ascended it 'from the fox's earth to the hawk's nest,' and on April 15, 1892, a party containing several of the same members climbed 'the first main gully on this [the north] side. There are two short chimneys at the end of this little gill—one in each corner, about ten to twelve yards apart.' The left one, up which Mr. Brunskill led, was considered the harder. Afterwards Dr. Collie led two of the party up the face of the cliff to the right of the next gully on the west, which is marked by a pitch of about fifty feet low down. To a house near the foot of Buckbarrow old Will Ritson and his wife retired, after giving up the inn which they had kept for so many years and made so famous at *Wastdale Head.*

Buresdale, the proper name of the valley between Thirlmere and Threlkeld. Hutchinson, for instance, says : 'At the foot of *Wythburn* is *Brackmere* [i.e. Thirlmere], a lake one mile in length. . . . from the N. end of this mere issues the river Bure, which falls into Derwent below Keswick.' He also mentions Buresdale in connection with *Layswater,* yet another equivalent for Thirlmere. Guidebook writers seem to have conspired together to obliterate this name from the map, and to substitute for it the name *Vale of St. John,* which Sir Walter Scott made famous. To revive the name of the river would be an act of only posthumous justice, now that the Manchester waterworks have taken away all its water ; but the valley is still there, and ought to be called by its genuine old name, which is of Scandinavian origin ; compare with it the Bure river in Norfolk, and fishermen will recall similar names in Norway.

Burn : the Scotch word for a brook is hardly found south of the river Wear. In Wythburn, Greenburn, and other cases it probably represents *borran* (stone heap).

Buttermere, a pleasant stopping-place from which many of the Cumberland fells can be explored. It is a good centre for *Grassmoor, Melbreak* and the *Red Pike range,* while *Borrowdale* and *Ennerdale* are quite within reach. Once a day the Keswick waggonettes swoop upon the place, bringing trippers by the score, but at other times it is a quiet and enjoyable spot.

Calf (The) (2,220 ft.), in Yorkshire, near *Sedbergh. Cautley Crag,* on the E. side of it, is very steep. In this corner of the county the Yorkshire climber experiences the intense relief of seeing rocks which are neither chalk, limestone, nor millstone grit.

Camping.—Camping out by rivers has always been more popular in England than the same form of airy entertainment among the mountains. The labour of carrying tents or sleeping-bags acts as the chief deterrent. It is true that some thirty years ago a distinguished member of the Alpine Club applied to Scafell Pike, and one or two other spots where England is loftiest, the practice, which he has carried out on many of the higher peaks of the Alps and Pyrenees, of watching sunset and sunrise from the loftiest possible *gîte* which the mountain can afford. Mr. Payn, too, has given us a most humorous narrative of how he and his friends encamped on Fairfield. Also, about twenty years ago, four stalwart climbers from Penrith made a regular camping tour of the Lakes. Their tent was pitched on these spots: Penrith Beacon, Red Tarn on Helvellyn, in Langdale under Pike o' Stickle, Sty Head, in Ennerdale under Gable Crag, and on Honister. It weighed only 5½ lbs., and yet had a floor space of 8 ft. by 8 ft.

It may be that, just as bicyclists suffered by the scathing definition 'cads on casters,' so the enthusiasm of the camper may have received a check when he heard himself described with cruel terseness as 'a fool in a bag.' Perhaps, again, our climate is not one which offers much encouragement to any but the hardiest of campers. In the Lakes by far the most popular (and probably, therefore, the most convenient) place

c

is the shore of Ullswater, where tents have been seen even in the depth of winter.

Carl Crag lies on the sea-shore in Drigg parish. Mr. Jefferson says that it is of syenite, and measures in feet twelve by nine by five and a half, but it is deep in the sand. The legend is that while Satan was carrying it in his apron to make a bridge over to the Isle of Man, his *apron strings* (*q. vid.*) broke and let it fall. It is probably an erratic. With the name compare *Carlhow, Carlwark*, &c.

Carrs, in Lancashire, in the *Coniston* range, north of the *Old Man*. It is craggy on the east side. In *Far Easdale* there is a line of crag which bears the same name. Clearly neither can have anything to do with ' carrs ' in its usual sense in the north, viz. ' low marshy ground.'

Castle Rock (C. sh. 64).—This rock in *Borrowdale* is said to have been crowned by a Roman fort. The west side is craggy for a couple of hundred feet. It may serve to occupy a few odd hours for any one stopping at *Grange, Rosthwaite*, or *Seatoller*.

Caw Fell (C. sh. 73).—The name is possibly the same as *Calf, Calva* ; compare also *Caudale, Codale*, &c. On the north side there is a craggy bit about 200 ft. high.

Chalk.—Though this can hardly be regarded as a good rock for climbing, much excellent practice can be gained on it. As a general rule, it is only sufficiently solid for real climbing for the first twenty feet above high-water mark, though here and there forty feet of fairly trustworthy rock

CHALK CLIFFS NEAR DOVER

m ιy bɔ found. These sections of hard chalk are invariably
those which at their base are washed by the sea at high tide;
all others are soft and crumbly.

Whilst any considerable ascent, other than up the extremely steep slopes of grass which sometimes clothes the
gullies and faces, is out of the question, traverses of great
interest and no slight difficulty are frequently possible for
considerable distances. A good *objectif* may be found in the
endeavour to work out a route to the various small beaches
that are cut off from the outer world by the high tide and cliffs.

The best instances of this sort of work are to be found
along the coast to the eastward of Dover (between that town
and St. Margaret's). Between the ledges by which these
traverses are in the main effected, and the beach below,
scrambles of every variety of difficulty may be found, some
being amongst the hardest *mauvais pas* with which I am acquainted. Owing to the proximity of the ground, they afford
the climber an excellent opportunity of ascertaining the
upper limit of his powers. Such knowledge is a possession
of extreme value, yet in most other places it is undesirable to
ascertain it too closely. Chalk, it must be remembered, is
extremely rotten and treacherous, very considerable masses
coming away occasionally with a comparatively slight pull.
In any place where a slip is not desirable, it is unwise to
depend exclusively on a single hold, as even the hardest and
firmest knobs, that have stood the test of years, give way
suddenly without any apparent reason. The flints imbedded
in the chalk are similarly untrustworthy; in fact, if they
project more than an inch or so, they are, as a rule, insecure.

The surface of the chalk is smooth and slimy if wet, dusty if dry, and does not afford the excellent hold obtained on granite. As a whole it may be regarded as a treacherous and difficult medium, and one which is likely to lead those practising on it to be very careful climbers.

To the westward of Dover (between it and Folkestone) a great amount of climbing on grass and crumbly chalk slopes can be obtained ; almost every gully and face can be ascended from the sea, or the S. E. Railway, to the top. It is desirable to remember that in dry weather the grass and the earth which underlies it is of the consistency of sand, and great care is requisite ; after rain the grass is of course slippery ; but the underlying material adheres more firmly to the cliff. It is unnecessary to add that a slip on any of these slopes would almost certainly prove fatal. On the face of *Abbot's Cliff*, and to the westward (about halfway between Dover and Folkestone), some traverses may be effected at a height of 200 ft. or more above the base ; they do not, however, compare for climbing with the traverses on the other side of Dover.

As one goes westwards, the angle of the cliffs becomes less, and from *Abbot's Cliff* towards Folkestone it is rarely necessary to use one's hands, though very nice 'balance' is essential, as the results of a slip would usually be serious. Above the *Warren*, still nearer Folkestone, the slopes become easy, and after heavy snow afford excellent *glissades*.

The cliffs between Dover and St. Margaret's vary from 200 to 350 ft., whilst those between Dover and Folkestone vary from 250 to 500 ft. in height.

In Sussex the chalk is well developed at and near *Beachy Head*, where it attains a height of some 600 ft. Just west of this come several miles of cliffs, lower indeed (about 300 ft.), but amazingly vertical.

About *Flamborough Head*, in Yorkshire, this formation attains fine proportions, while as far west as Devonshire *Beer Head* is upwards of 400 ft. high.

Chimney : a recess among rocks resembling the interior of a chimney open on one side. (See *Back-and-knee*.)

Chockstone : a northern word for a stone wedged between the sides of a gully. A short word for this is greatly needed, and I would suggest that it might be called a ' chock,' simply.

Clapham, a station on the Midland Railway, is an excellent centre for *Ingleborough* and the *Potholes*.

Clark's Leap, near *Swirl's Gap* on Thirlmere, is a jutting rock, so called from a suicide which took place there over 100 years ago. It is one of many local absurdities of the novel called ' The Shadow of a Crime ' that this name is brought in as an antiquity in the eyes of characters supposed to be living two centuries ago.

Clough (*Cleugh, Cloof, Cluff, Clowe*) is a North of England word for a kind of valley formed in the slope of a hill. The first cut in carving a shoulder of mutton produces a typical ' clough.' There is seldom any climbing about a genuine clough, because it implies soil rather than rock. Dr. Murray tells us that the word has no connection with the Icelandic ' klofi,' yet assigns to the latter word the origin of ' cloof,' in the sense of the fork of a tree, or of the human body. To a layman in such matters the two words bear a singular resemblance, both in sound and in sense.

Collier's Climb on *Scafell* was made by Messrs. Collier and Winser on April 2, 1893, and a very severe climb it is. It begins from the *Rake's Progress* at a point 105 ft. west from the *North Climb*. After a direct ascent of about 40 ft., a grassy platform on the right (facing the wall) is reached. From here a narrow and somewhat awkward traverse leads back to above the first part of the climb. This traverse could probably be avoided by climbing directly up-wards. There follows an easy ascent for 30 ft. still directly upwards. By traversing broad grassy ledges to the right—i.e. towards *Moss Gill*—one of the inclined cracks so plainly seen on the face of the cliff is reached, and the rest of the ascent made in it. The only severe difficulties in the climb are: 1. at the beginning, in leaving *Rake's Progress*; 2. at one point in the crack where there is not much handhold for 10 or 15 ft.

Combe Gill, a fine gill in the north end of *Glaramara*. The climb is a little over two miles from *Rosthwaite*, and about a mile less from *Seatoller*. A very fine mass of rock (one of the many *Eagle Crags*) stands at the head of the little valley, and up the centre of this crag lies the way. It was climbed on September 1, 1893, by Messrs. J. W. Robinson and W. A. Wilson, whose account of it is as follows: ' This very fine gorge has three good-sized pitches in the lower part. These were passed by climbing the right-hand edge of the gill—interesting work. A return on to the floor of the gill was made near the top of the third pitch, when a little scrambling led to a very fine waterfall more than 100 ft. high Here climb in the water as little as you can; then diverge slightly on to the right-hand wall of the gill just where the water spouts over a small recess ; next traverse across a rather difficult slab into the cave under the final boulder, which is climbed on the left-hand and is the last difficulty.'

Coniston, having the advantage of both railway and steamboat, is very accessible, and, notwithstanding this, it is agreeably free from the rush of excursionists.   Practically it has one fine mountain—the *Old Man*—and no more, though *Bow Fell* and the *Langdale Pikes* are not entirely out of reach.   There is much good scrambling in the rocks which fringe the *Old Man* and *Wetherlam*, and superb climbing in *Dow Crag*.

Coniston Old Man.—Quarrymen and miners have between them done an immense deal towards spoiling a very fine mountain.   They have converted to base industrial uses the whole east side of the mountain, which Nature intended for climbers.   They have not yet invaded *Doe Crag* (q.v.), which is really part of it, but practically no one goes up the *Old Man* proper, except for the sake of the view, which is magnificent, and no one ascends except from Coniston, varied in a few cases by working north along the summit ridge and descending viâ *Grey Friars* on to the pass of *Wrynose*.

Copeland.—Camden says of Cumberland: ' The south part of this shire is called *Copeland* and *Coupland*, for that it beareth up the head aloft with sharpedged and pointed hilles,

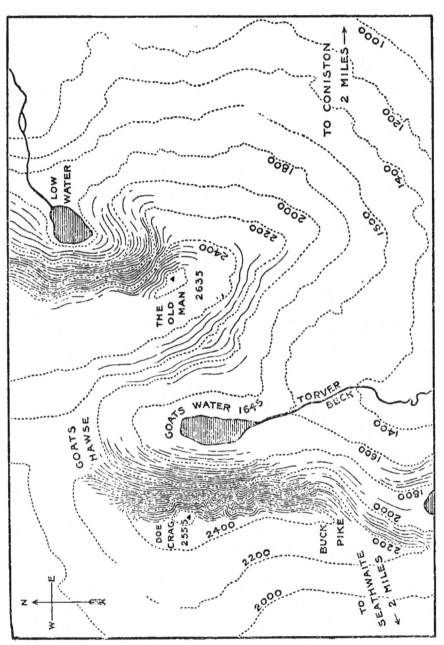

CONISTON AND DOE CRAG

which the Britans tearme *Copa.*' Leland alludes to this when
he makes a ludicrously pedantic suggestion : ' Capelande, part
of Cumbrelande, may be elegantly caullid Cephalenia.' *Cop*
is found in Derbyshire also, as a hill-name, and hunting men
will not need to be reminded of the Coplow in Leicestershire.

Cornwall.—To the true-souled climber, who can enjoy
a tough bit of rock, even if it is only fifty, aye, or twenty feet
high, the coast of Cornwall with its worn granite cliffs and
bays has much to offer. It is interesting almost the whole
way round the coast. Granite prevails, but at Po*lp*err*o* we
have cliffs belonging to the Lower Devonian period, and for
some ten or twelve miles going west from *Chapel* Po*int* we
find rocks of the Silurian order. At many points round
the *Lizard Promontory* there are remarkable rocks ; but
some of the finest cliff scenery in England is to be found
between the *Logan Rock* and the *Land's End.* These are
on the regular tourist tracks, and conveniently reached from
good hotels ; but the north coast of Cornwall is here easy of
access. There are fine cliffs about *Gurnard's Head* and
Bosigran, which are well worth a visit, from St. Ives or
Penzance (7 or 8 miles). There is a small inn at *Gurnard's
Head.* *Bedruthan Steps* are well-known, and *Trevose Head,*
Pentire (Padstow), *Tintagel* and *Penkenner* Point are only
a few of the many grand rock-scenes on this coast.

Coterine Hill.—Leland, in his ' Itinerary,' says that
Ure, Sawle, and Edon rise in this hill, and that ' the Hedde
of Lune River by al Aestimation must be in *Coterine Hill,*
or not far fro the Root of it,' adding that, in the opinion of

Mr. Moore of Cambridge, the river Lune 'risith yn a hill cawlled *Crosho*, the which is yn the egge of Richemontshire.'

There is *Cotter-dale* on the Yorkshire slope of the hill in which these rivers rise, and the celebrated Countess of Pembroke, in 1663, when she crossed from *Wensleydale* to *Pendragon Castle*, calls her journey 'going over *Cotter*, which I lately repaired,' the last words showing that it was a recognised pass.

In all probability Leland's form represents ' *Cotter End*,' by which name, though not given in most of the maps, part of the hill is still known.

Cove : often means ' cave ' in Yorkshire and Scotland, but as a rule it is a large recess in a hill-side.

Craven. —*Camden* remarks that the country lying about the head of the river Aire is called in our tongue *Craven*, ' perchance of the British word *Crage*, that is a *Stone*. For the whole tract there is rough all over, and unpleasant to see to ; which [with ?] craggie stones, hanging rockes, and rugged waies.'

Modern climbers, however, find it hardly rocky enough for them, at least above ground, and have been driven to invent a new variety of climbing—the subterranean. Exploration of the numerous *potholes* which honeycomb the limestone hills has of late years become a favourite pastime, and, in truth, it combines science with adventure to a marked degree.

Any one who tarries for any length of time among these Yorkshire dales should read Mr. H. Speight's handsome volume, which gives a very complete account of the beauties and the curiosities which they have to show.

Cross Fell, in Cumberland, long enjoyed the reputation being one of the highest mountains in England, and as late as 1770 its height was calculated at 3,390 ft., which is some 500 ft. more than it is entitled to. It was earlier than most English mountains in becoming the object of scientific curiosity, and an account of it will be found in the *Gentleman's Magazine* for 1747. It is chiefly celebrated for the Helm Wind originating from it.

Cumberland is the premier climbing county. The best centres are *Wastdale Head*, *Rosthwaite* or *Seatoller*, *Buttermere*, *Keswick* and *Eskdale*. The cream of the climbing is on those fells which are composed of rocks belonging to what is called ' the Borrowdale Series,' such as *Scafell Pillar*, *Gable*, *Bowfell*, and as a rule the finest climbs are found on the sides which face the north and east. *Cross Fell* does not belong to the same mountain-system as those just mentioned, and offers little climbing. The best cliffs on the coast are about *St. Bees* Head.

Cust's Gully, on Great End.—To the large and increasing number of men who visit the Lakes in winter, perhaps no climb is better known than this. In the spring of 1880, a party, including one of the greatest of lady mountaineers, and over twenty members of the Alpine Club, ascended this ' very interesting chimney or couloir, which, being filled with ice and snow, gave unexpected satisfaction. There is a very remarkable natural arch in this couloir, which

Mr. Cust claims to have been the first to discover, and he was therefore entrusted with the guidance of the party.' The orthodox approach is by way of Skew Gill, which is conspicuous at the right hand on nearing Sty Head from Wastdale. A short distance beyond the head of this gill our gully is seen rising on the right, marked by the conspicuous block of stone. Being, as the Scotch say, 'back of the sun,' this gully often holds snow till comparatively late in the season. Indeed, in winter, it is sometimes so much choked with snow that the arch disappears, and it is even said that self-respecting climbers, who recognise that a gully ought to be followed with strictness, have felt bound to reach the block by tunnelling, instead of walking over the top. In the spring of 1890 there was a tremendous fall of stones, by which the gully was nearly filled. Except in snow time, loose stones are an objection, and many find it more interesting to ascend by a small gully, almost a branch of ' Cust's,' on the right hand. As climbs neither of them will compare with the more eastern gullies.

Dale : curiously used in Derbyshire for each separate section of a river valley, which elsewhere would form only one dale.

Dalegarth Force, in Cumberland, near Boot, in Eskdale. The wall on the north side of this extremely pretty little fall is very low ; but, being granite, offers one or two problems to the climber. *Stanley Gill* is another name for the same place.

Dartmoor, a high upland moor, forming a vast reservoir, from which most of the Devonshire rivers are fed. It is curious rather than beautiful, and more interesting to the geologist, the antiquary, and the fisherman than it is to the mountaineer. Yet it is instructive even to him, for the frequency of rain and mist and the paucity of landmarks which can be seen more than a few yards off, coupled with the necessity of constantly watching the ground, render it one of the easiest places in the world in which to lose one's way in any but the finest weather. There are no true hills, but here and there a gradual rise of the ground is seen, with a lump or two of granite grotesquely planted on the top of it. These are the *Tors*. As a rule they are very small, but often present problems to the climber, and are seldom without interest of some sort.

A great many may be reached from Tavistock or the little inn at *Merivale Bridge*.

Dead Crags (C. sh. 56) are lofty but disappointing rocks on the north side of Skiddaw. There is perhaps 500 ft. of steep crumbly rock, something like *Hobcarton*.

Deep Gill.—The name is not infrequent; for example, there is one on the south side of *Great Gable*, east of the *Napes*, but now it is always called *Hell Gate*. *The* Deep Gill is on *Scafell*, and falls into the *Lord's Rake*. The first mention of it was made in August 1869 by Mr. T. L. Murray Browne, who wrote in the Visitors' Book at Wastdale Head: ' The attention of mountaineers is called to a rock on Scafell on the right (looking down) of a remarkable gill which cleaves the rocks of Scafell and descends into Lingmell Gill. It looks stiff.' The rock alluded to is the *Scafell Pillar* and

DEEP GILL, SCAFELL
(The Lower Pitch)

the gill is *Deep Gill*. It is well described by Mr. Slingsby
in the *Alpine Journal*, vol. xiii. p. 93 : 'After a couple of
hundred steps had been cut in the snow in Lord's Rake and
at the bottom of Deep Gill, which joins the former at right
angles, we reached the first block—a large rock perhaps
15 ft. square—which overhangs the gill, and so forms a cave.
Below the rock the snow was moulded into most fantastic
shapes by occasional water-drips from above. At the right
hand of the big rock a few small stones are jammed fast
between it and the side of the ravine, and they afford the
only route up above the rock. These stones can be reached
from the back of the little cave, and occasionally from the
snow direct. Hastings—who is a very powerful fellow and a
brilliant climber—and I got on the stones, as we did last
year. He then stood on my shoulder, and, by the aid of
long arms and being steadied by me, he reached a tiny ledge
and drew himself up. Mason and I found it no child's play
to follow him with the rope. Some two hundred more steps
in hard snow brought us to the only place where we could
attack the second block. Here three fallen rocks stop the
way, and on the left hand is the well-nigh ledgeless cliff
which terminates far away overhead in the Sca Fell Pinnacle,
or Sca Fell Pillar. On the right a high perpendicular wall
effectually cuts off the gill from the terraces of Lord's
Rake. On the left hand of the gill a small tongue of rock,
very steep, juts out perhaps 40 ft. down the gully from the
fallen block nearest to the Pinnacle wall, and forms a small
crack, and this crack is the only way upward. From a
mountaineer's point of view the stratification of the rocks

here is all wrong. The crack ends in a chimney about 20 ft. high, between the wall and a smoothly polished boss of rock. Hastings, still leading, found the crack to be difficult, but climbed it in a most masterly way. All loose stones, tufts of grass and moss, had to be thrown down, and, in the absence of hand and foot hold, the knees, elbows, thighs, and other parts of the body had to do the holding on, whilst, caterpillar-like, we drew ourselves upward bit by bit. The chimney is best climbed by leaning against the Pinnacle wall with one's back and elbows, and, at the same time, by walking with the feet fly-like up the boss opposite. From the top of the boss a narrow sloping traverse, perhaps 12 ft. long, leads into the trough of the gill. With a rope this is an easy run ; without one it would not be nice. A stone thrown down from here falls over both blocks and rolls down the snow out of the mouth of Lord's Rake on to the screes far away below. The crack, chimney, and traverse, short distance though it is, took us about an hour to pass. The climb from Deep Gill to the gap from which the Pinnacle is ascended is a very good one, which two men can do much better than one. The Pinnacle itself from the gap is perhaps 25 ft. high, and is really a first-rate little climb, where the hands and the body have to do the bulk of the work.'

The date of Mr. Slingsby's attempt was March 2, 1885, and that of his successful ascent March 28, 1886: but as early as 1882 this climb had been made, piecemeal, by the present writer, who, however, never, so far as he can remember, blended the different items into a continuous climb until the summer of 1884, when he descended the whole length of

D

the gill in company with Mr. Chr. Cookson, of C. C. C., Oxford. A yet earlier descent of the gill had been made at Easter 1882 by Messrs. Arnold Mumm and J. E. King, of the same college, who found such a phenomenal depth of snow that the obstacles were buried, and they were able to walk from end to end without using their hands. The same thing happened again in January 1887, when Messrs. Creak and Robinson were able to walk up over both pitches without having even to cut a step.

The lower pitch may also be passed by using a recess resembling one half of a funnel in the red rock of the vertical south wall of the gill. The worst part of this is where you leave the funnel and begin to coast round in order to re-enter the gill. The space comprised between the two pitches can be entered very easily by passing round the foot of the *Scafell Pillar*, or with much more difficulty down the vertical south wall. The upper pitch may be passed in two ways, besides the incline. One is by means of a narrow side gully, the upper stage of which is most easily passed by following the ridge which divides it from the main gill. The third way is the most direct and the most difficult, lying between the incline and the great block. Mr. Owen Jones seems to have invented it in the year 1892, and took up a party by it on that occasion with the assistance of a good deal of snow, and another party in the month of August 1893, when there was no snow at all. There is no more fashionable winter climb than *Deep Gill*, and about Christmas time the clink of the axe echoes among its crags from dawn to dusk.

It is reached from Wastdale Head in about an hour and a half. The shoulder of *Lingmell* has first to be rounded, and it makes little difference either in time or fatigue whether this be done comparatively high up or by taking the high road to the bridge near the head of the lake or by an intermediate course. At any rate, a long grind up *Brown Tongue*, in the hollow between *Lingmell* and *Scafell*, cannot be avoided, and when the chaos called *Hollow Stones* is reached a vast outburst of scree high up on the right hand indicates the mouth of *Lord's Rake*. After a laborious scramble up this scree the rake is entered, and only a few yards further the lower pitch of Deep Gill is seen on the left hand.

Deep Gill Pillar.—See *Deep Gill* and *Scafell Pillar.*

Derbyshire is well endowed in point of rock scenery, but it is not really a climber's country. The rocks are of two kinds—the Limestone, of which Dovedale may be taken as a type, and the Millstone Grit, which prevails further north. The former shows many a sharp pinnacle and many a sheer cliff, but is often dangerously rotten, while the latter assumes strange, grotesque forms, and, when it does offer a climb, ends it off abruptly, just as one thinks the enjoyment is about to begin. It is, nevertheless, much more satisfactory than the limestone, and many pleasing problems may be found on it, especially in the neighbourhood of the *Downfall* on *Kinder Scout*. For this Buxton or Chapel-en-le-Frith is ot course a better centre than Matlock.

Devonshire.—The inland climbing in this county is very limited. Of granite there are the *Tors* of Dartmoor and the Dewerstone near Plymouth, and there is a remarkably fine limestone ravine at Chudleigh, but there is little else worthy of mention. But the coast of Devonshire is exceptionally fine, and perhaps no other county can show such a variety of fine cliffs. At *Beer Head* we have chalk; at *Anstis Cove*, *Torbay*, and *Berry Head* limestone; at *Start Point* and *Stoke* Point slate. For bold cliff scenery few parts of the Channel can rival the piece between *Start Point* and *Bolt Tail*.

On the north coast of Devon there are many striking cliffs. Among them may be noticed *Heddon's Mouth*, *Castle Rock* (at Lynton), some rocks about Ilfracombe, the granite cliffs of *Lundy*, *Hartland* Point; in fact much of the coast from Clovelly right away to Bude in Cornwall is remarkably fine.

Dixon's Three Jumps, on Blea Water Crag (High Street, Westmorland), so called from the famous fall here of a fox-hunter about the year 1762.

Perhaps no one ever fell so far and yet sustained so little permanent injury. As an instance of 'the ruling passion strong in death,' or at least in appalling proximity to death, it may be mentioned that, on arriving at the bottom, he got on his knees and cried out, 'Lads, t' fox is gane oot at t' hee eend. Lig t' dogs on an' aa'l cum syun.' He then fell back unconscious, but recovered, and lived many years after.

Another Dixon fell while fox-hunting on Helvellyn in 1858, but was killed. There is a monument to him on Striding Edge.

Dodd : a round-topped hill. The word is common in the Lowlands and in the North of England. It is often said to mean a limb of a larger mountain, but Dodd Fell in Yorkshire would alone refute this, being the highest hill in its neighbourhood.

Doe Crag, in Eskdale (C. sh. 74), is a bold rock, long reputed inaccessible, low down on the north side of the approach to *Mickledoor* from the east. The Woolpack in Eskdale is the nearest inn. The rock, as a climb, is very inferior to its namesake at Coniston (see *Dow Crag*).

Door Head, the *col* between *Yewbarrow* and *Red Pike*. There is capital scree here, and a very rapid descent into Mosedale may be made by it. Men who have spent the day on the Pillar sometimes return to Wastdale Head round the head of Mosedale, and wind up by racing down these screes from the *col* to the stream below. The distance is about 650 yards, and the perpendicular drop about 1,200 ft. Anything less than five minutes is considered very ' good time.'

Doup : any semicircular cavity resembling half an egg-shell (N. of Eng.).

Dow (or **Doe**) **Crag,** in Lancashire, lies just west of *Coniston Old Man*, being only divided from it by *Gout's Water*. The climbing here is second to none. There are three or four superb gullies. Perhaps the best is in a line with the head of the tarn and the cairn on the *Old Man*, and another scarcely, if at all, inferior is nearly opposite a

DOE CRAG, CONISTON

The lowest pitch of the central gully. The top of the wedged block is reached
by mounting the shallow scoop on the left of the picture, and then coasting
round into the gully again.

very large stone in the tarn. The first ascent of one was made by Mr. Robinson and the writer in the year 1886; that of the other by a party including Messrs. Slingsby, Hastings, E. Hopkinson, and the writer in July 1888. The last-mentioned (with indispensable aid from the rope) afterwards descended an intermediate gully of terrific aspect.

Towards the foot of the tarn the gullies are much less severe.

Above is an illustration of the first pitch of the gully climbed in 1888. Mr. Hastings led up the shallow crevice seen on the left of the picture, and on reaching the level of the top of the pitch contoured the intervening buttress into the chimney again. This is no easy matter and required great care.

Dunald Mill Hole.—One of the earliest descriptions of a ' *Pothole* ' will be found in the ' Annual Register ' for 1760, where this curiosity is treated of at some length. It is a good specimen of a common type, and lies between Lancaster and Carnforth.

Dungeon Gill, in Langdale, deserves mention in any treatise on British climbing, inasmuch as the poet Wordsworth has made it the scene of an early deed of daring performed by an idle shepherd boy—

> Into a chasm a mighty block
> Hath fallen and made a bridge of rock,
> The gulf is deep below.

The gulf and the mighty block are both there still; but there

is more pleasure in seeing the former than there is excitement in crossing by the latter.

Eagle Crag.—Rocks of this name are pretty numerous
in the North of England, and, like the ' Raven Crags,' are, as
might be expected, always bold and precipitous.

On Helvellyn.—Canon Butler, in his article on the Lakes
in 1844, which appeared in *Longman's Magazine*, describes
in an amusing manner an adventure which he had on this
rock. It is on the right-hand side of the track from Patterdale to Grisedale Hause.

In Easdale (W. sh. 17).—This is easily found by following up the stream which runs into Easdale Tarn. There
is not more than 200–300 ft. of crag, and much of it is very
rotten, but with pretty bits of climbing here and there.
Grasmere is the only place from which it is conveniently
reached.

In Greenup (C. sh. 75) is as noble a rock as can be found
in England. As seen from Borrowdale near Rosthwaite it
has the appearance of two huge steps of rock, but the steps
are really separate rocks, one behind the other—Eagle
Crag and Pounsey Crag. Large portions of each of them
are quite unclimbable, and much of them is too easy to
be worth doing, so that the amount of interesting climbing
to be met with is less than might be expected. Close by is
Longstrath, where there is a little work which may be com-
bined with this (see *Blea Crag* and *Serjeant Crag*). The foot
of Eagle Crag is reached from Rosthwaite or Seatoller in
less than an hour,

Eagle's Nest—one of the ridges of the *Napes* lying between the *Needle* and the *Arrowhead*. On April 15, 1892, Messrs. Slingsby, Baker, Solly, and Brigg ascended it and found it extremely difficult for 150 ft. At one point, about on a level with the top of the *Needle*, there is room for one person to sit down, and here the second man on the rope joined the leader and gave him a shoulder up. To this place they gave the name of the *Eagle's Nest*, and it is almost the only point at which any material help can be given to the leader.

The part just above this they considered the stiffest part of the climb; but when they reached a patch of grass just below a slanting chimney the difficulties moderated. From the bottom to where the ridge joins the *Needle Ridge* they took two hours and ten minutes.

Eel Crag.—The word 'Eel,' we are told, is identical with 'Ill,' which is seen in *Ill Bell* and the numerous *Ill Gills*, and means 'steep.' If so the name ought to be more frequent in the Lake country than it is, and it might be suggested that in some cases 'eagle' may have been worn down to 'eel.' There are two crags of the name in Cumberland, not very far apart.

In Coledale.—These rocks are steep, but too much broken up to be really worth a visit on their own account. However, after *Force Crag* has been tried, these are conveniently near.

In Newlands (C. sh. 70).—Among the rocks which flank Newlands on the east much good material may be found.

One is reminded a little of the Wastwater Screes, but of course these are not on anything approaching that scale. The greatest height of the craggy part is only about 400 ft.

Eight-foot Drop.—On the Pillar Rock is the passage from the ridge of the *Curtain* down on to the lower part of the *Steep Grass.* It figures in some of the earlier accounts as a formidable feature of the ascent. Nowadays it is known how much easier it is to keep on the flank of the curtain, and only leave it when at the top of the chimney which runs up from the head of *Steep Grass.* No 'drop' is, in fact, necessary ; but the climb, though not in any sense difficult, is generally regarded as a good test of neatness of style.

Ennerdale.—For a valley which not only is one of the largest and most impressive in the Lake country, but contains moreover a share of the most perfect mountain in broad England—Great Gable—and all of the most famous rock—the Pillar—singularly little is popularly known of Ennerdale. But, when we consider that the place is one which is, or should be, hallowed to all devout Wordsworthians as the scene of one of the finest productions of their poet, the thing becomes incomprehensible. To begin with, the guide-books have never done it justice. In area of paper covered with descriptions of it English Lakeland is probably many square miles ahead of any equal portion of the earth's surface. But guide-book writers love to stand upon the ancient ways ; and any one who takes the trouble to compare West or Otley with the works of to-day must admit that, except in matters of detail, the advance has been incredibly small. The public are better judges of accuracy than of enterprise, and what pleases the public pays. These gentlemen, therefore, worthy and painstaking as they are, share to some extent in the narrow aspirations of the hireling, and, indeed, we are tempted to believe that their motives in shunning Ennerdàle were not wholly foreign to the character of him who 'fieeth because he is afraid,' for they have brought up a terrible report of the dale. If, however, this has been a wise precaution on their part, a means of deterring any inquirer from exposing their want of energy, it has been rewarded with a large measure of success. Here is an inviting prospect for a timid traveller : ' Ennerdale Lake . . . . is so wild in the character of its shores and in its position among the mountains as to have caused more terrors and disasters to strangers than any other spot in the district. At every house from Wastdale Head to Enner- dale Bridge stories may be heard of adventures and escapes of pedestrians and horsemen in Mosedale and the passes of Black Sail and Scarf Gap ' (Whellan's ' History of Cumber- land,' 1860). Can it be wondered at that, in the face of such terrors as this, very few people find their way into Ennerdale, except those who with fear and trembling cross the head of it on their way between Buttermere and Wastdale Head ? Every guide-book, indeed, mentions Ennerdale and the Pillar by name, because it gives an opportunity for quoting the well-worn lines from ' The Brothers,' after which a few meagre remarks may be expected to follow on the ' Pillar Moun- tain,' the ' Pillar Rock,' and ' Ennerdale Lake,' expressions of which not one, strictly speaking, is correct, for the proper name of the first is beyond all doubt ' Pillar *Fell*,' ' mountain ' being an innovation of tourists and guide-book writers, who between them have made ' Pillar *Rock* ' sound more familiar than the genuine name ' Pillar *Stone*,' and have almost ousted ' Broadwater ' in favour of ' Ennerdale Lake.'

Printed authorities are scanty, because Ennerdale is of very recent discovery. The early guide-books simply know nothing about it. West (1778) does not mention it, and the gifted authoress of that touching poem ' Edwina ' did not even know how to spell its name :

> But chiefly, Ennersdale, to thee I turn,
> And o'er thy healthful vales heartrended mourn,
> Vain do thy riv'lets spread their curving sides
> While o'er thy glens the summer zephyr glides.

And yet Mrs. Cowley was by no means indifferent to such points. Indeed, we owe the origin of this exquisite poem to her etymological zeal and to her desire to immortalise the brilliant suggestion that the name ' Wotobank ' was derived from some one having once said, ' Woe to this bank ! ' It may even be that the spelling is a symbolical subtlety—a kind of refinement on ' word-painting ' intended to shadow forth to less poetic minds, by the sinuosity of the superfluous ' s,' the unique manner in which the rivulets of this happy valley are wont to ' spread their curving sides.' One of the earliest visitors to Ennerdale appears to have been the artist Smith, of Derby (1767), who sketched the lake, as did also Wilkinson in 1810. Wordsworth had been there before 1800, and Green's description shows that he was much struck by the scenery of upper Ennerdale. But, though visitors to Ennerdale have been and still are few, most of these few speak highly of its

beauties, ' partly perhaps,' says Mr. Payn, ' in consequence of
their having endured certain inconveniences (with which they
are anxious that you should also become acquainted) when
belated in that lovely spot.' The dale is not without its associations. Formerly it was a deer forest, the property of the
Crown by forfeiture from the father of the ill-fated Lady
Jane Grey. The Sandford manuscript speaks enthusiastic-
ally of ' the montaines and fforest of Innerdale, wher ther is
reed dear and as great Hartts and Staggs as in any part of
England. The bow-bearer is a brave gentleman.' But it is
now many years since the last of the herd was destroyed, and
no one living can remember the days when Ennerdale could
show—what in almost any landscape is a crowning beauty—
the stately figure of a great red stag. Certainly an element
of romance has here been lost ; but how can that be felt so
long as here and there some aged man survives to keep green
among the dalesmen the memory of ' t' girt wild dog ' ? The
stories told of this remarkable animal would fill volumes and
form a highly interesting study in contemporary mythology ;
and yet, when we consider the state of unparalleled excitement into which the whole countryside was thrown at the
time, and the assiduity with which it has ever since been
talking over the events of that stirring period, we shall find
cause to wonder, not that the story in some of its details should
have acquired a slight legendary flavour, but rather that the
great bulk of the incidents narrated should be so thoroughly
well authenticated. Certainly it is a lesson in faith, and
makes it easier to credit stories such as that which Ovid tells
with so much spirit of the Calydonian boar ; for if in the days

of modern firearms a dog can defy a large district and kill a couple of sheep a day for nearly half a year together, there is less reason for doubting that in old days an amount of destruction and devastation which would not discredit a modern minister could be wrought by the unaided exertions of one malevolent pig. For months the dog was hunted and shot at, but seemed to lead a charmed life; in the excitement farming operations were terribly neglected, until at last, in the person of John Steel of Asby, arose the modern Meleager.

Many a story is told of that exciting time, and one especially has hit the fancy of the dale. Until recently the custom was that fox-hunts should take place on one particular day of the week—a day the selection of which for a Southern meet would, however convenient, be regarded with considerable surprise. Possibly this custom was held to govern dog-hunting also; for one Sunday, as the Rev. Mr. Ponsonby (probably the identical 'homely priest' who is mentioned in 'The Brothers') was conducting Divine Service, the attentive ears of the congregation caught the sound of some commotion without, followed by the rush of hounds and the panting of human lungs. There could be no mistaking these signs. A faint murmur passed round the sacred building, 'T' girt dog!' and in an instant the reverend gentleman was the only male within the walls. A moment's pause, and then female sympathy and female curiosity triumphed, and the other and better half of the congregation disappeared. The story goes in Ennerdale (but for this we decline to vouch) that the aged pastor, casting a sorrowful glance upon the empty benches, hastily adjusted the robes of his office, and ere the last petticoat had fluttered from the porch was in full career to join the headlong hunt.

For five months Ennerdale had been in a state of con- vulsive excitement, for the first and last time, it is said, ' syn t' Flud '; the honour of having enlivened the dale is fairly divided between the Deluge and the Dog.

To see Ennerdale as it should be seen, and to get a clear idea of the surrounding district, there is no better plan than to mount from Buttermere to Red Pike—the Rigi of Cum- berland—and from there follow with eye and, if necessary, map the following account of a 'run,' telling how ' oald Jobby o' Smeathat tallyho't a fox ya Sunday mworning, just as day brak, oot ov a borran o' steeans, abeunn Flootern Tarn, i' Herdas end; an' hoo it teukk ower be t' Cleugh gill an' t' hoonds viewt him sa hard 'at he teuk t' Broadwater an' swam 'cross t' hee end on't, an t' dogs went roond an' oop t' Side Wood . . . an' they whisselt him oop be t' Iron Crag, an' be t' Silver Cwove an then throo t' Pillar, an' a gay rough bit o' grund it is. ' Hoo he shakt 'em off a bit theer, an' they at him agean an' meadd o' ring amang t' rocks. Hoo they ran him roond be Black Sail, an' Lizza hee faulds an' clam oot be t' Scarf Gap an' on to t' Wo' heead an' they beeldit 'am onder t' Brock Steeans an' he was seaff aneugh theer.'

With or without the fox-hunt this view from Red Pike is magnificent, yet there are several others which run it very close. What, for instance, can be better, just at the clearing of a shower, than the look-out from the Pillar Fell on the opposite side of the valley? From the gloom and grandeur around it the eye travels right along to the smiling green of the open country beyond the lake bordered by a line of glittering sea. This view has one drawback in that you cannot at one time be looking both from the Pillar and at it; but then it is hardly possible to enter Ennerdale at all without seeing this rock, the real glory of the valley, from many effective points; and, moreover, no day there is complete without a quiet half-hour spent in floating on the lake about sunset; for, whether it be due to the westerly lie of the dale or to some other cause, the fact remains that the Ennerdale sunsets are not to be beaten among the Lakes. By the early morning light the upper part of the valley should be explored, and the marvellous view enjoyed from Haystacks : from the 'bulky red bluff of Grasmoor' on the right to the dark recess of Mosedale half seen upon the left all is beautiful ; separated from Crummock and Buttermere, which are both well seen, by the steep Red Pike range, Broadwater throws in a dash of life to relieve the desolation of upper Ennerdale, while the richly coloured screes of Red Pike sweep down in striking contrast to the forbidding frown of the Pillar Fell. We have seen a fine water-colour sketch which renders this view with great fidelity. It has additional interest as the work of the first amateur who ever scaled the Pillar Stone— Lieut. Wilson, R.N.

The scenery of Ennerdale, however, would not long have remained beautiful if the Ennerdale Railway Bill, promoted in 1883 and 1884, had been suffered to pass into law. That scheme was happily defeated, and the only modern touches added to the dale have been the galvanised wire railings recently erected along the sky-line, and the blue indicators set up on the Black Sail and Scarf Gap track.

Eskdale.—There are two dales of the name in Cumberland, but the only one which is of interest to mountaineers is reached by the little railway from Ravenglass. Lodgings, largely used by Whitehaven people, are to be had, but the most convenient inn is the Woolpack, about a mile up the valley from the terminus of the line. From no place can *Scafell*, *The Pikes*, or *Bow Fell* be more easily explored, while the Coniston range is quite within reach, and the Wastwater *Screes* are more accessible than they are from Wastdale Head. The valley itself is only second to Borrowdale, and there are grand falls and deep pools in the Esk. There are also some good rocks, though not quite equal to the description of Hutchinson, who says that 'Doe Cragg and Earn Cragg are remarkable precipices, whose fronts are polished as marble, the one 160 perpendicular yards in height, the other 120 yards.' Both of these will be seen on the way up to *Mickledoor*, the former standing on the right-hand side at the foot of the steep ascent. It is strange that so few climbers ever go to this valley.

Esk Pike, a name given by the shepherds to a peak of 2,903 ft., which stands at the head of the Esk valley. Being left nameless by the Ordnance six-inch map, it has attracted to itself the nearest name it could find, and is very commonly called *Hanging Knot*, which, in strictness, applies only to the north shoulder of Bow Fell, where it hangs over Angle Tarn. It would save some confusion if this name had a wider cur-

E

reney than it has.   At the head of Eskdale there is a rather
good gully, which was climbed at the end of September 1892
by Messrs. Brunskill and Gibbs, whose account of it is that
' its direction is W.N.W., and it consists first of a short pitch
of about 10 ft.; then a slope of 20 ft. at an angle of 60°–65°,
the holds in which are fairly good ; and, last, another pitch
at a somewhat similar angle, with an awkward corner of rock
to round.   Above this to the top is an easy scramble.'

Fairfield (2,863 ft.), in Westmorland, sometimes called
Rydal Head in old books, stretches down to Grasmere and
Ambleside; but it is from Patterdale that it should be seen
and climbed.   One of the best things on it is *Greenhow End*,
which stands at the head of Deepdale. The steep part, which
is not wholly crag, is 400 or 500 ft. high, and faces N.E.

This is the mountain which Miss Martineau so greatly
longed to ascend, and every one knows Mr. Payn's account of
how he encamped upon it.

There is another *Fairfield* in the Coniston Fells.

Falcon Crag, a couple of miles from Keswick, beside
the road to Borrowdale, is not more than 150 or 200 ft.
high, but at many points so vertical as to be quite unclimbable.
The steepest side is also the most exposed to the public gaze.
On the south side there is a deep gully in which excellent
scrambling is to be had.

Fellpole is a much better word than its foreign equivalent, ' alpenstock ' Except in the depth of winter on the
highest fells it is of much more use than an axe, which is, of
course, indispensable when there is much snow or ice.   On

difficult rocks either axe or pole is a great incumbrance; but where there is much scree, or steep grass, or broken ground, all three of which abound on the Fells, a pole is a very great comfort on the descent. Of course, while being used for this purpose, it must be kept behind the body. On the steep nose of *Fleetwith* a fatal accident occurred to a young woman solely in consequence of her attempting to descend with her stick held improperly in front of her. This is a fault which nearly all beginners commit. Nevertheless, it is perfectly legitimate to use the pole in that way if it is to break the force of an abrupt drop from rest to rest—as, for instance, when a slope is broken into binks separated by drops of from three to six feet. In such cases a jump is often dangerous, and the life of Mr. Pope, lost on *Great Gable* in 1882, is only one of many which have been similarly sacrificed.

Force Crag is reached from Keswick by way of Braithwaite station and the long *Coledale* valley. Here the track of the disused mining tram is a well-engineered road direct to the foot of the crag, where the fragments of the baryta mine are littered about. The best climb is up to the basin, into which pours the force, and then, leaving the force on the right, ascend a steep, dry gully. The rock is very treacherous, being not only loose, but covered with long fringes of rotten heather. It is very difficult to get out, as the top part steepens rapidly. The force is very fatal to sheep. On one occasion the writer counted no less than six of their carcasses in the basin.

Froswick.—It is most easily reached from Staveley or Windermere by following up the valley of the Kent, or from

Ambleside by crossing the Garbourn Pass into the same valley. This hill resembles *Ill Bell* and *Rainsborrow Crag* in character, and has a very steep face towards the north-east, 300 or 400 ft. high. It is on sheet 20 of the Ordnance map of Westmorland.

Gaping Gill Hole, in Yorkshire, on the south side of *Ingleborough*, is most easily got at from Clapham, on the Midland Railway. It lies higher up than the well-known *Clapham* or *Ingleborough Cave*, and both should be visited in the same expedition. The actual funnel is about 8 ft. by 20 ft., and Mr. Birkbeck, of Settle, partly descended it many years ago. There is a ledge of rock about 190 ft. down, from which a plumb-line drops a further distance of 166 ft. Strangers often pass close to the place without finding it.

Gash Rock.—We are indebted to Colonel Barrow for this name, which he bestowed on *Blea Crag* in Langstrath apparently for no better reason than that he knew a man called Gash, who did not know the name of the rock, or how to climb it.

This rock is the ' spy-fortalice ' spoken of in Prior's Guide. It is an upstanding block of squarish outline, conspicuous on the left hand as one ascends Langstrath from Borrowdale. It is climbed from the side which faces down the valley, and is rather a stiff little rock of its inches.

It was climbed by Mr. Owen Jones and Mr. Robinson on September 6, 1893, but there is some doubt whether it had not been done before (see *Blea Crag*).

Gavel—apparently the local form in the North of England of the Southern 'Gable.' In the older maps 'Great Gable' is usually spelt in this way, and for part of that mountain the name *Gavel Neese* (i.e. nose) still lingers among the shepherds. Generally speaking, in the less frequented parts, where the names are used only by the shepherds, we find this form. Thus we have *Gavel Fell* between Loweswater and Ennerdale, *Gavel-pike* on St. Sunday Crag, *Gavelcrag* on the south end of *High Street*, and again on *Seat Sandal*, and this form is used in the Lowlands of Scotland, while on the more frequented *Skiddaw* we get *Gablegill.* In Icelandic, 'gafl' is said to mean 'the end of a house or of a ship.'

Gill (or *Ghyll*).—In a large part of the North of England this is the regular word for a stream flowing between walls of rock. It is by many regarded as a test-word for Scandinavian settlements, and it is certainly more abundant in such districts, but notice should be taken of the fact that in Kent it is applied to the steep wooded slopes of a brook-valley. There is good authority for both spellings, but the less romantic of the two is to be preferred.

Gimmer Crag, just behind the inns at *Dungeon Gill* in *Langdale*, has good scrambling on it. Mr. Gwynne says of it : ' Between *Harrison Stickle* and the *Pike o' Stickle*, commonly called the *Sugarloaf*, there is a splendid crag that is full of opportunities. This fine piece of rock, although it has the appearance of being easy, has the disadvantage of being wet, and therefore more or less dangerous. However, there are times even in the Lake District when the rain ceases and the sun shines, and it is then that the climber should gambol upon this crag.'

Glaramara—a long broken hill stretching from Stonethwaite along the east side of Borrowdale to Esk Hause. Its name is only less disguised than its nature in the description given of it in the 'Beauties of England,' p. 65 : 'Glamarara is a perpendicular rock of immense height.' Sir W. Scott has confused it with *Blencathra*. It contains very little climbing' but *Combe Gill* and *Pinnacle Bield* may be mentioned.

Gordale Scar—a magnificent limestone ravine near *Malham Cove*, in Yorkshire, on the line of the great Craven Fault. Bell Busk is the nearest station, but Settle (6 miles) is generally more convenient. It has been prosaically compared to a winding street between enormously high houses, with a river falling out of the first-floor window of one of them. It is easy to pass out at the head, leaving the water on the right hand; but on the other side of the water there is quite a little climb, which, however, the writer has seen a lady do without assistance.

Goyal.—This west-country word for a gully will not require explanation for readers of Mr. Blackmore's 'Lorna Doone.'

Grain : the northern word for a prong, and hence the usual name for the branches of a stream.

Grassmoor (2,791 ft.) in the older maps and guide-books (such as Robinson's) is often called Grasmere or Grasmire.

The only climbs which it presents are on the side which drops steeply down towards the foot of Crummock Water, and the only inns within a convenient distance are at Scale Hill (1 mile) and Buttermere (3 miles). There are two gullies which furrow the mountain side nearly from top to bottom. The more southerly of these has two pitches in it close to the foot, and the upper of the two is generally thought as hard as anything on the mountain. The approved method of doing it is to keep the back to the rock until the top of the pitch is nearly reached, and then to break out on the south side. Above this pitch the gully is of little interest. The north gully is of more sustained merit, but, as seen from below, less prominent, and therefore easily overlooked. It may, however, be recognised by its liberal output of scree. It has three pitches near the foot, and in all three the hold is somewhat scanty. The first forms a narrow gully rising from left to right, and is the highest and hardest. Higher up than these a broad wall of rock some 40 ft. high cuts across the gully and gives a pretty climb. Above the wall there is a branch to the left containing one little pitch, but the main channel continues. Loose stones are now the only source of excitement, and climbers are recommended to get out to the right and finish the ascent along the rocky ridge of the bank. It is very safe climbing on this face, yet full of interest and instruction, and for the initiation of a 'young hand' nothing could be better.

Great End (2,984 ft.) has not received justice at the hands of the Government map-makers, who have scamped their work most shockingly. The six-inch map would lead the innocent stranger to imagine that he could ascend from Sprinkling Tarn by a smooth and gradual slope. The cliffs are on the right-hand side on the way from Sty Head to Esk Hause, and are reached from Wastdale or Borrowdale by way of Sty Head, and from Langdale by Rossett Gill. The best general view is from Sprinkling Tarn. Col. Barrow, when citing Great End in his book as an instance of a mountain with one impossible side, no doubt refers to these cliffs, which, however, long before he wrote, had been climbed in every direction. He might reasonably object to *Cust's Gully*, invented in 1880, as being quite at the end of the cliff; but from a point some way below the foot of that gully there is an easy passage, sloping up the face of the cliff very much like Jack's Rake on *Pavey Ark*, and this passage was descended by Mr. Cust in the same year that he discovered the gully. A little later a couple of ardent fox-hunters got into difficulties in one of the main gullies, and so drew more attention to these rocks. The whole face was pretty thoroughly explored by the present writer in the summer of 1882. Two very fine gullies face Sprinkling Tarn. *Great or Central Gully*, the nearer of the two to *Cust's*, is also the wider, but not quite so long as the other. It has a copious scree at the foot, and more than half-way up it divides into three. The central fork is grassy, that to the right is more abrupt, while the left-hand way lies for several yards up a wet slide of smooth and very steep rock. On the slide itself there is hold enough for comfort; but on getting off it at the head to the left hand there comes a bit on a disgustingly rotten buttress which even good climbers have often found very unpleasant. Above this the

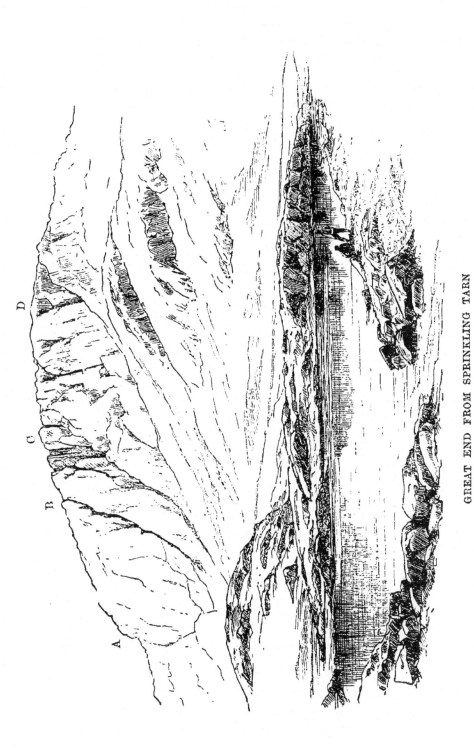

GREAT END FROM SPRINKLING TARN

A, Position of *Brigg's climb* (not seen) ; B, The east gully ; C, The great central gully ; D, *Cust's gully.*

gully is more open and very easy, but splendid climbing may
be had on either side of it.

The South-East Gully, as it is usually called, has its
mouth only some 20 yards east from that of the last.   Being
much narrower, it is bridged by numerous ' choke-stones,' and,
while less fine than the other in snow time, offers in summer
a better and rather longer climb.   Half-way up or less there
is a fork, the dividing ridge forming quite a sharp *aréte.*
Above it the forks coalesce, and as it nears the top the climb
can be varied a good deal.

Brigg's (or *Holmes'*) *Pitch,* of which a photograph will be
found in the Climbers' Book at Wastdale Head, is still nearer
to Esk Hause, which it faces.   Mr. Holmes and the Messrs.
Brigg, who climbed it on Easter Monday 1893, describe the
difficulty as consisting in a cave formed quite at the foot of
the cliff by a jammed stone, the top of which is reached by
way of the rocks on the north side of it.

Great Gable (2,949 ft.) may be ascended with equal
ease from Wastdale or the head of Borrowdale, and is within
easy reach of Buttermere.   The simplest way up is by
Sty Head, from which half an hour's rough walking lands
one on to the top.   The only alternative for Wastdale is
' Moses Sledgate,' alias *Gavel Neese,* a ridge of rather steep
grass, which offers a very direct way.   There is a bit of
scrambling on White Napes, a rocky mass which tops the
Neese.   Beyond this *Westmorland's Cairn* is left on the right
hand and the summit cairn comes into sight.   People coming
from Buttermere usually go round the head of Ennerdale

over Green Gable, and this is the way generally taken by
Borrowdale visitors for the return journey. The climbing on
this mountain is quite first-class. The *Napes, Napes Needle,*
and *Kern Knotts* are separately described, but in addition to
these there are grand crags overlooking Ennerdale. These

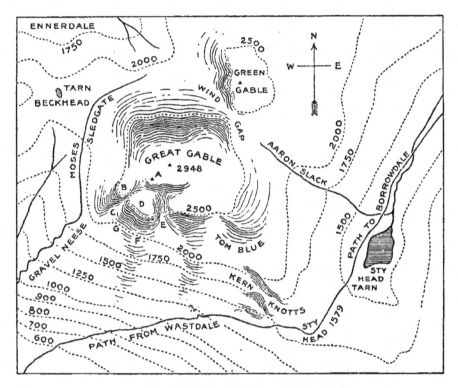

PLAN OF GREAT GABLE

A, *Westmorland's Cairn* ; B, *White Napes* ; C, E, *Little and Great Hell Gate* ;
D, *Great Napes* ; F, *Napes Needle.*

are referred to in Col. Barrow's book in the passage where he
defies the Alpine Club to ascend the most difficult side of
certain Lake mountains.

No one seems even to have looked at these crags till in

1882 Mr. Pope met his death on this side of the mountain.
In that year the writer found that it was an easy matter to

GREAT GABLE FROM THE SOUTH-EAST

A, *Kirkfell* ; B, *Beckhead* ; C, *White Napes* ; D, *Great Napes* ; E, *Westmorland's Cairn* ; F, Summit ; G, *Tom Blue* ; H, *Kern Knotts.*
The path to *Sty Head* is seen mounting from left to right.

coast along the face of the cliff at about two-thirds of the height of it, and a year or two later that for all the ferocious appearance of these rocks there is a natural passage by which a mountain sheep of ordinary powers might ascend them. Close to this are the remains of a sort of hut of loose stones, evidently the refuge of some desperate fugitive of half a century or more ago. Local tradition speaks of a notorious distiller of illicit whisky, who was known to have a 'hide' somewhere in this wild neighbourhood. The top of the easy passage bears by prismatic compass 23° from the highest cairn, and is marked by a large stone.

To the east of this spot there is fine climbing, the rocks being on a grand scale and difficult on that account. At intervals large masses are detached by such agencies as frost, and heavy falls result. One of these carried with it a slab pinnacle which, though only about 15 ft. high, was remarkably difficult. The writer, and Messrs. Hastings and Robinson gave themselves the trouble of climbing it, and consequently heard of its untimely departure with deep regret.

In April 1890 Mr. J. W. Robinson greatly assisted subse-quent climbers by inserting a sketch in the Wastdale Head book, and this sketch has been the usual basis of later work.

Gable has the threefold excellence of being splendid to look at, splendid to look from, and splendid to climb; and one can easily understand the enthusiasm of Mr. F. H. Bowring, who has ascended it over one hundred times.

Green Crag.—A good piece of rock, though not as sound as it might be, at the head of *Warnscale*, the recess between *Fleetwith* and *Scarf Gap*. It is reached from Buttermere

by way of Gatesgarth, and then by the quarry track which
goes up on the south side of Fleetwith to *Dubs*.   There is a
fine gully in the crag which is unmistakable.   A note of the
ascent of it was made by Messrs. J. W. Robinson and W. A.
Wilson in August 1889.

Griff—a valley-name in east Yorkshire, probably connected with ' greave,' which is common in Derbyshire.
Phillips says that the Yorkshire word means ' a narrow, rugged
valley.'

Gurnard's Head, in Cornwall, not far from St. Ives,
is a fine promontory on which there is good climbing.   It is
here that the greenstone ends and the granite begins, pre-
vailing from this point practically right on to the Land's End.

Hanging Knot.—See also *Esk Pike.*   The steep breast
above Angle Tarn contains no continuous climb, but there
are several good bits in the rocks and gullies which con-
nect the terraces.

Hard Knot.—' Eske,' says Camden, ' springeth up at
the foote of *Hardknot*, an high steepe mountaine, in the top
whereof were discovered of late huge stones and foundations
of a castle not without great wonder, considering it is so steepe
and upright that one can hardly ascend up to it.'

This refers of course to the Roman camp, which is
nowhere near the top.   The ' mountaine ' scarcely deserves
the name ; it is not high, and though rugged offers no climbing.
Writers much later than Camden refer to it as if it were one
of the highest hills in England.   Even Gray, in his *Journal*,

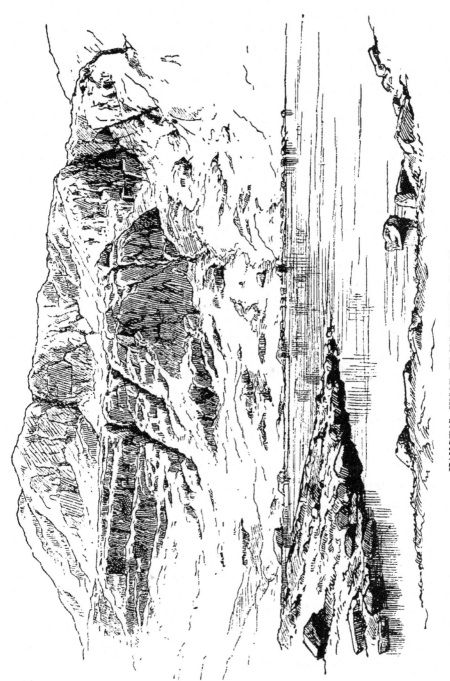

HANGING KNOT FROM ANGLE TARN

says 'Wrynose and Hardknot, two great mountains, rise above the rest.'

The usually accurate West introduces in the funniest way both 'the broken ridge of Wrynose' and 'the overhanging cliff of Hardknot' into his description of the view from Belle Isle on Windermere, and says that they, with others, 'form as magnificent an amphitheatre, and as grand an assemblage of mountains, as ever the genius of Poussin,' &c.; and then adds a note to say that they 'are named as being in the environs, and are in reality not seen from the island.'

Harrison Stickle, 'the next neighbour of *Pavey Ark*, is another happy hunting-ground for beginners. There are at least four good routes up. There is one to the north-east which is fairly difficult. Due south there are two or three rather steep gills, that may be climbed with a certain amount of ease. But in no case should the climber, even on the easiest of these routes, omit to use the rope and take every precaution against preventable accidents.' Thus speaks Mr. Gwynne in the *Pall Mall Gazette*, and to his remarks little need be added, except that it must be borne in mind nothing on this group is quite in the same class as *Pavey Ark*. The obvious starting-point for either is Dungeon Gill at the very foot, where there are two inns, but Grasmere is within easy reach, being only about an hour further off.

Hause (*hass, horse, -ourse, -ose*) : used in the North for a pass. The word means 'neck' or 'throat,' the latter being the sense most felt in local names, where it refers more to lateral contraction than to vertical depression, being thus parallel to *gorge* rather than to *col*.

Haystacks, just east of Scarf Gap, has one craggy bit on it where, as appears from the curious map published in the *Gentleman's Magazine* for 1751, eagles then built. The name is often quoted as an instance of the Norse word which occurs in *Stack Polly,* and frequently on the Scotch coast, but West says it was called *Hayrick* (*sic*) on account of its shape.

Hell Gate.—A channel on *Great Gable,* just by the east end of the *Napes.* It is the outlet for immense quantities of scree. The older name, *Deep Gill,* has during the last twenty years being quite supplanted. The present name, if less pretty, is more precise, and saves confusion with the better known *Deep Gill* on *Scafell.*

Hell Gill.—There are many gills and becks bearing this name. Speaking of one in Yorkshire, Leland says it is 'a Bek called Hell Gill because it runnithe in such a deadly place. This Gill commithe to Ure.' The idea is amplified by Camden : 'Where Richmondshire bordereth upon Lancashire amongst the mountaines it is in most places so vast, solitary, unpleasant and unsightly, so mute and still also that the borderers dwelling thereby have called certaine riverets creeping this waic " Hellbecks." But especially that about the head of the river Ure, which having a bridge over it of one entier stone falleth downe such a depth, that it striketh in a certaine horror to as many as looke downe.' The best known Hell Gill, which at one time had considerable reputation as a climb, is quite near the foot of *Bowfell* on the Langdale side. Though on a small scale, it is highly picturesque. The south

F

fork is hardly passable in ordinary weather owing to a small waterfall, below which is a deep pool flanked by perpendicular walls of rock, and except in very dry seasons it is necessary to crawl up the red rotten slabs, steep, slimy, and wet, which form the north fork. The gill should be visited more often than it is, as it is directly on one of the best ways up the mountain from Dungeon Gill and Langdale generally.

Helm Crag.—Colonel Barrow, speaking of this hill, observes that climbing among these rocks requires care. There are places quite as dangerous and as difficult as on any rock-work on the Alps. He was deterred from climbing the rock which is supposed to resemble a mortar, by a slab of rock slanting sideways, but in his opinion there was no great difficulty, except that arising from the absence of hold for hand and foot—an exception of some importance.

Helvellyn.—A mountain which belongs equally to Grasmere and to Patterdale, though the latter has by far the finest side of it. *Striding Edge* on this side was at one time considered to present terrors such as the hardy mountaineer was not likely to encounter elsewhere. This side is cut up into deep coves, which are exceedingly steep and afford many opportunities for scrambling, and near the path in Grisedale there is one of the numerous *Eagle Crags*.

On the west side there is no climbing on the mountain itself, but on the range of *Dodds*, which runs away to the north, there is capital work to be found; see *Bram Crag* and *Wanthwaite Crags*. It was in connection with Helvellyn that Colonel Barrow issued his famous challenge to the Alpine Club. After stating that he had ascended the mountain by every possible way of getting up it, and that it is the easiest of mountains to ascend from any direction that is possible, he continues : ' No one, I think, will venture the impossible, which may be found on all the highest mountains in the Lake District. They have their precipitous sides for adventurous climbers, who, I promise, will never get up them even if they have a mind to try—viz., these, *Great Gable*, *Great End*, *Helvellyn*, *Fairfield*, &c. Most of the difficult things in the Alps have been accomplished. Here is a new field for any of the adventurous climbers of our club : let them try these precipitous sides ! ' Helvellyn was long regarded as the loftiest of the Lake mountains, the height assigned to it by West being 3,324 ft., and even its tame grassy slopes towards *Wythburn* were thought very terrible indeed. In the 'Beauties of England' Thirlmere is described as ' a scene of desolation which is much heightened by the appearance of the immense craggy masses, that seem to hang on the sides of Helvellyn, from whose slopes they have apparently been severed, but arrested in their tremendous progress down the mountain by the impulse of gravitation. Huge and innumerable fragments of rocks hang pendant from its sides, and appear ready to fall and overwhelm the curious traveller who dares to ascend its wild and fantastic heights.'

Heron Crag, Eskdale.—A rock in *Eskdale* (q.v.) which was long reputed inaccessible. It was supposed to be 120 yards high, and to have a front like polished marble. It will

F 2

be found north of the Esk river, not far from *Throstlegarth*
(Cumberland, sheet 79).

High Level.—This name was bestowed about the year
1880 on a particular route, by means of which the north-east
foot of the *Pillar Rock* may be reached from *Black Sail*
along the face of the mountain, thus avoiding the descent
into Ennerdale and the subsequent laborious ascent to the
rock. The saving in time is very considerable, but the way
is so easily missed in thick weather that a stranger who
attempted it would probably gain nothing but an exciting
walk.

After reaching the slight hollow between *Lookingstead*
and *Pillar Fell*, *Green Cove* is seen below. Here a descent
may be made at once, but it is better to proceed westward
till about two dozen uprights of the iron railing are passed,
and then to descend, keeping as much to the left as the cliffs
will allow. The whole art of choosing a line along this face
is to cross each successive cove as high up as may be done
without getting impeded by rocky ground. The ridges which
separate the coves mostly form small headlands, and just
above each headland a strip of smooth grass crosses the
ridge. Economy in time is usually of more importance at
the end than at the beginning of a day, and it is well to know
that, whereas from the foot of the rock to *Black Sail* by
way of the valley would take up the greater part of an hour,
Mr. Hastings and the writer once timed themselves on the
High Level, and found that they reached *Lookingstead* in
18 minutes and the ford in Mosedale in seven minutes more.

High Stile, in Cumberland, between Ennerdale and Buttermere, has a height of 2,643 ft., and on its north-west side a few good crags. It is best reached by following up the course of *Sour Milk Gill* from the foot of Buttermere to *Bleaberry Tarn*, which can be reached from any of the inns in an hour's walking. In a note made in the Wastdale Head book in August 1887, Mr. Robinson called attention to these rocks, and he it is who has done most of the exploration here.

The principal climbing is in and about a gully in the centre. A course may be taken up very steep grassy binks with the gully on the right hand. The gully itself was climbed direct in September 1893 by Messrs. Jones, Robinson and Wilson, and they found the second pitch very difficult. The same party also ascended 'a short, black-looking chimney away round on the left of the great crag, and nearer the top of the mountain.' The very hard upper pitch was passed on the right hand, and the final pull was by the arms alone. Both climbs are in full view from Rigg's Buttermere Hotel.

The mountain is called *High Steel* in some early maps, and in that of the Ordnance it comes on sheet 69.

High Street, with the Roman road running all along its ridge, lies between Patterdale and Mardale Green, in Westmorland. It has a fine precipitous side towards the latter place at Blea Water (see *Dixon's Three Jumps*), and at the south end of it, about Gavel Crag and Bleathwaite Crag, there are some good rocky faces, which can be readily found by following up the course of the beck from Kentmere.

Hobcarton Crags have a considerable repute, which they have only retained by reason of their not being very easily got at. The simplest way of reaching them from Keswick is to take the train to Braithwaite, then go up the straight Coledale until Force Crag is passed, then trace the stream which comes down the hill on the right. Hobcarton is just over the ridge, and the crags are on the left-hand side of the valley. A descent may be made of a ridge which forms the right bank of a gill, which runs from near the *col* where you are now standing; the gill itself is too rotten.

The *Crags* are very steep and very rotten; but there is one curiosity about them, in the shape of a continuous sloping ledge, growing very narrow indeed towards the top. It rises gradually in the direction of *Hopegillhead*. The crags are picturesque, but can be traversed in any direction without difficulty, and present no definite climb. Another way of reaching them from Keswick is by crossing Whinlatter Pass, and on the far side turning up the first valley to the left hand.

Honister, one of the grandest crags in Cumberland, is reached from either Buttermere or Borrowdale. It is one of the chief attractions of the 'Buttermere Round' made by the breaks from Keswick. If quarrymen could only have been persuaded to let it alone, it would have been a delightful climbing ground; as things are, we can only look and long. Apart from the great crag there is a fine view of the lakes below from the summit (called *Fleetwith Pike*). Owing to its position near the black-lead mines, this was one of the earliest Lake mountains of which we have a recorded ascent. It was made before the middle of last century, and, so far as can be made out, these early mountaineers ascended from Seathwaite and passed to the northward of *Grey Knotts*, and so to the top of Fleetwith. 'The precipices were surprisingly variegated with apices, prominencies, spouting jets of water, cataracts and rivers that were precipitated from the cliffs with an alarming noise' [Sourmilkgill]. On reaching the apparent top, they were astonished to perceive a large plain to the west, and from thence another craggy ascent, which they reckoned at 500 yards. 'The whole mountain is called *Unnisterre* or, as I suppose, Finisterre, for such it appears to be.' In about another hour two of the party gained this summit— 'the scene was terrifying—the horrid projection of vast promontories, the vicinity of the clouds, the thunder of the explosions in the slate quarries, the dreadful solitude, the distance of the plain below, and the mountains heaped on mountains that were lying around us desolate and waste, like the ruins of a world which we only had survived excited such ideas of horror as are not to be expressed. We turned from this fearful prospect, afraid even of our- selves, and bidding an everlasting farewell to so perilous an elevation. We descended to our companions, repassed the mines, got to Seathwayte, were cheerfully regaled by an honest farmer in his *puris naturalibus*, and returned to Keswic about nine at night.'

Hope (-*hop*, -*up*): used by Leland as equivalent to 'brook,' but usually taken to mean a retired upland valley. The Icelandic 'hop' is applied to landlocked bays.

Hough—a hill name in east Yorkshire. Phillips says that it is equivalent to 'barf,' and means 'a detached hill.' It is pronounced 'hauf.' If this be the exact sense, it can hardly be the same word as 'heugh,' which is used further north for 'crag' or 'precipice,' and it is perhaps merely another form of 'how' or 'haugh.'

How (*-oe, -ah, -a, -haw*) : a Norse word for a burial mound, found all over the North of England.

Ice-axe.—On the high Fells in time of snow an axe is a safeguard of vital importance. Quite apart, too, from the comfort and security which it alone can give, it is an implement which can only be properly manipulated after long practice, and consequently a beginner should eagerly avail himself of every opportunity of acquiring dexterity in the use of it. From Christmas to Easter there is nearly always snow enough on the fells of Cumberland to give excellent practice in step-cutting.

Ill Bell.—A Westmorland hill forming a series of three with *Froswick* and *Rainsborrow Crag*. Its north or north-easterly face is very steep for a height of about 300 ft. Staveley is perhaps the best starting-point for these three ; but they can be managed quite easily from Ambleside or Mardale Green. *Ill Bell* is on sheet 20 of the Ordnance map of Westmorland.

Ingleborough, 2,361 ft., one of the most striking of the Yorkshire mountains, of which the poet Gray spoke as 'that huge creature of God.' Readers of the 'Heart of

Midlothian ' will remember how it reminded Jeannie Deans of her ' ain countrie.' The most exaggerated ideas of its height formerly prevailed. Even in 1770 it was commonly reckoned at 3,987 ft., and Hurtley actually gives 5,280 ft.

Its top is only about four miles from Clapham, and ponies can go all the way. It is ascended far and away more frequently than any other Yorkshire hill, and consists mainly of limestone cliffs and slopes of shale, with a certain amount of millstone grit.

Here are some very remarkable caves (see *Alum Pot* and *Gaping Gill Hole*), and of some of these there is an early description by Mr. Adam Walker in the *Evening General Post* for September 25, 1779, which is quoted by West, and an account of an ascent of it made in the year 1761 is also extant.

Jack's Rake is a natural passage across the face of *Pavey Ark* in Langdale. The first notice ever taken of it by any but shepherds was a note in the visitors' book belonging to the inn at Dungeon Gill by Mr. R. Pendlebury, who spoke highly of it, considering it to be a striking yet simple excursion among magnificent rock scenery. After a time the world came to look at *Pavey Ark*, and seeing an impossible-looking combination of ravine and precipice, concluded, not unnaturally, that it must be what Mr. Pendlebury had found a pleasant yet simple stroll. Under this delusion, they began to try to climb what is now known as the Great Gully in *Pavey Ark*, and did not expect to find a place anything like the real *Jack's Rake*.

Mr. Gwynne, in 1892, says of it : ' Along the face of the cliff there runs a ledge that looks from below hardly wide enough for a cat to stand upon.   However, if an attempt is made to climb it, it will be found wide enough for two fat men walking abreast.   Towards the top it tapers off again, and the climber will have to do a bit of scrambling to get on to the summit of the precipice.   This is a climb which offers no difficulty whatever, unless the climber is given to attacks of giddiness, and if that is the case there will hardly be any need to tell him that he has no business there at all.   This ledge, however, offers a multitude of good opportunities to the climber.   It runs obliquely across the face of the precipice, but it need not necessarily be followed throughout its length by the mountaineer who wishes for something a little more exciting.

'About halfway up there runs on to the ledge a chimney which, when it is not a small waterfall, forms a pleasant climb to some broken rock above, whence the summit is easily reached.   If, however, the water in the chimney makes it uncomfortable and unpleasant for the climber, he may still arrive at the top of it by choosing a long bit of steep smooth rock to the left.   There are two cliffs which afford fairly good hand and foot holds, and from there the top of the chimney is attained.'

It is remarkable that a gallery more or less resembling this is found on many of the chief precipices in the Lakes. There is a steeper one on the Ennerdale Crags of *Great Gable*; there are two on the Ennerdale face of the *Pillar Rock*, and on *Scafell* the *Rake's Progress* and *Lord's Rake* in their mutual

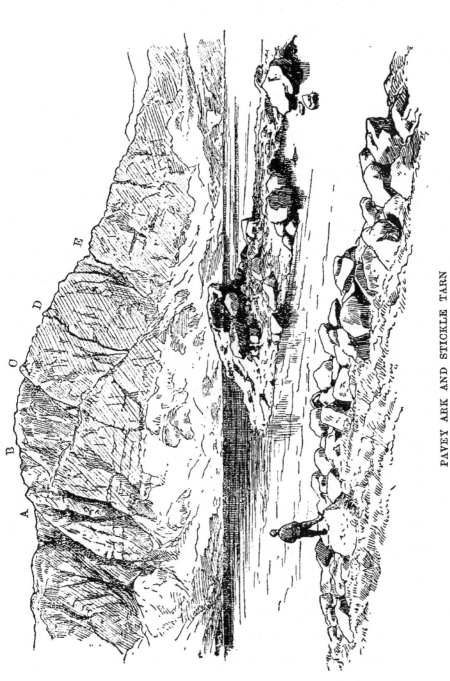

PAVEY ARK AND STICKLE TARN

A, Narrow gully; B, Big gully; C, D, Smaller gullies; E, Wide scree gully. From the foot of E to A runs *Jack's Rake.*

relation closely resemble this rake and the wide gully at the north end of it.

Kern Knotts are on the south side of *Gable*, close to the *Sty Head*. There is a short but difficult gully here on the side facing Wastdale, which was climbed by Messrs. Owen Jones and Robinson in 1893, but described by them under the name of *Tom Blue*, a rock much higher up the mountain.

Keswick.—Though rather too distant from the very best climbing, this is an excellent centre in point of variety.

Of *Skiddaw* and *Saddleback* it enjoys a monopoly, while *Helvellyn*, *Gable* and *Scafell Pikes* are all within the compass of a day's work. The railway is a convenience, of course, but not as useful as one might expect in extending the field of operations, because most of the places to which it goes are of little interest. The town is very well supplied with driving facilities, such as coaches, breaks and omnibuses.

The clay-slate of which the Skiddaw and Grassmoor groups are composed provides climbing of smaller quantity and inferior quality to that found among the harder rocks of what is called the 'Borrowdale Series,' but there are a few good scrambles west of Derwentwater, such as *Eel* (or *Ill*) *Crag*, *Force Crag*, and *Hobcarton*. The nearest good rocks are in the neighbourhood of *Wallow Crag*, but there is no pleasure in climbing with a crowd of gaping excursionists below. A much pleasanter day may be spent in a visit to *Wanthwaite*. Of Keswick itself an early writer says that the poorer inhabitants subsist chiefly by stealing or clandestinely buying of those who steal the black-lead, which they sell to Jews and other hawkers ; but whatever changes the character of the people has or has not undergone, it is not easy to believe that the scenery is the same as that which the early writers describe.

Camden's tone is neutral: 'Compassed about with deawy hilles and fensed on the North side with that high mountaine *Skiddaw* lieth *Keswike*; ' but two centuries later, when the place began to be fashionable, this description would not have satisfied any one. The great characteristic of the scenery was considered to be its power of inspiring terror. Dr. Brown in his famous ' Letter ' dwells upon the ' rocks and cliffs of stupendous height hanging broken over the lake in horrible grandeur, some of them a thousand feet high, the woods climbing up their steep and shaggy sides, where mortal foot never yet approached. On these dreadful heights the eagles build their nests, . . . while on all sides of this immense amphitheatre the lofty mountains rise round, piercing the clouds in shapes as spiry and fantastic as the very rocks of Dovedale. . . . The full perfection of Keswick consists of three circumstances, *beauty*, *horror* and *immensity* united.'

Kirkfell has two fine buttresses of rock at the back, facing Ennerdale, but they are broken up and so only fit for practice climbs. They are, however, not unfrequently assailed by climbers who imagine themselves to be scaling the crags of Great Gable. The direct ascent from Wastdale is one of the steepest lengths of grass slope to be found among these hills. The only gully on this fell is *Illgill*, which faces *Lingmell* and contains two or three severe pitches. It is rather seldom visited, and is exposed to falling stones.

Lancashire.—Though some of the rough country which borders on Yorkshire contains a rocky bit here and there, Lancashire climbing has no real interest except in that part of it which belongs to the Lake country. The climax of this part is reached in the neighbourhood of *Coniston*. South of the Lakes there are some limestone crags of striking form. The impression produced on Defoe by what we consider the exceptionally beautiful scenery of the Lune valley is curious. ' This part of the country seemed very strange and dismal to us (nothing but mountains in view and stone walls for hedges ; sour oatcakes for bread, or clapat-bread as it is called). As these hills were lofty, so they had an aspect of terror. Here were no rich pleasant valleys between them as among the Alps ; no lead mines and veins of rich ore as in the Peak ; no coal-pits as in the hills about Halifax, but all barren and wild and of no use either to man or beast.'

Langdale.—(See *Bowfell*, *Pavey Ark* and *Pike o' Stickle, Gimmer Crag, Harrison Stickle, Oak How.*) By many thought the finest valley in Westmorland ; the name is often written Langden or Langdon by old authorities.

Dungeon Gill has always been a favourite haunt of climbing folk, and from this base strong walkers can easily manage to reach *Scafell, Gable, Coniston, Old Man*, or *Helvellyn* in the day.

Limestone is abundant in Derbyshire and Yorkshire, and forms the fine cliffs of Cheddar in Somerset, Berry Head in Devon, Anstis Cove and others; indeed most of the south coast of Devon and Cornwall east of Penzance is of this material. Chudleigh Rock and Morwell Rocks on the river Tamar are very striking. West, speaking of this rock in Lancashire, says, 'The whiteness and neatness of these rocks take off every idea of *horror* that might be suggested by their bulk or form.' In England it is very rare to find lime-stone which is a satisfactory material on which to climb.

Lingmell, called *Lingmoor* by Wilkinson, is a mere shoulder of Scafell Pike. It has, however, some fine cliffs facing those of *Great Napes* on Gable; between these two Housman thought a collision imminent. These used to be thought inaccessible, but were climbed by Mr. Bowring about 1880. There is a striking view of them from near Sty Head. The eye looks right along the dark ravine of Piers Gill, which is apparently overhung by the long line of these crags, rising from tongues of rock divided by huge fan-shaped banks of scree. There is a good deal of chance about the climbing here. It may be exciting, or you may just happen to avoid what difficulties there are. It is a very treacherous rock, especially low down, where curious long stone pegs are lightly stuck in the ground and come away at the first touch. A few feet below the top stands a curious pinnacle of forbidding appearance, of which a sensational photograph has been taken; but Mr. Robinson found one side from which the top is reached with ridiculous ease. Further west there are gullies facing Kirkfell which are worth climbing, though there is much unsound rock.   (See also *Piers Gill.*)

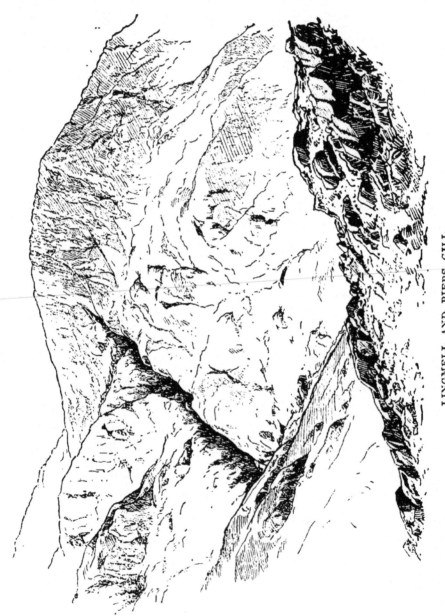

LINGMELL AND PIERS GILL

Lingmoor, rather over a mile south-east of Millbeck Inn, and near Oak How, is a little pinnacle of which a photograph and a description by Mr. H. A. Gwynne will be found in the Climbers' book at that place. In old maps the name is sometimes found applied to *Lingmell.*

LORD'S RAKE AND RAKE'S PROGRESS

A, The foot of *Moss Gill* ; B, The foot of *Steep Gill* ; C–D, *Lord's Rake* ;
C–A, Part of *Rake's Progress.*

Lord's Rake.—A well-known scree-shoot in the north face of Scafell, for the ascent of which from Mickledoor it offers an easy route without climbing. The earliest account of its being used for this purpose is in the *Penny Magazine* for 1837 at p. 293 : 'It is very laborious and looks dangerous, but in fact there is no risk except that of a sprained ankle. It is through the Lord's Rake, a shaft between two vertical walls of rock about five yards across all the way up, and twenty or twenty-five minutes' hard climbing on all fours up a slope of about 45°. The place must have been cut out by a watercourse, but is now dry and covered with light shingle. It looks right down into Hollow Stones (the deep vale between the Pikes and Scafell), and most fearful it does look, but it is not dangerous. When we reached the inn at Eskdale over Scafell my shepherd was very proud of having brought me through the Lord's Rake, and the people were much surprised. It seems to be rather a feat in the country. It is the strangest place I ever saw. It may be recommended to all who can bear hard labour and enjoy the appearance of danger without the reality.' 'Prior's Guide' contained the first good description of this rake.

Luxulion, in Cornwall, is of interest to the mineralogist and the travelled mountaineer on account of its enormous block.

According to Mr. Baddeley, this is the largest block in Europe, larger than any of the famous boulders at the head of the Italian lakes, and it may take rank with the largest known, the Agassiz blocks in the Tijuca mountains near Rio Janeiro. He gives the dimensions as 49 feet by 27 feet with 72 feet girth, yet makes no allusion to the *Bowder Stone* in *Borrowdale,* which in another work he describes as being 60 feet long, 30 feet high, and weighing 1,900 tons. It would appear, therefore, that the *Bowder Stone* is considerably larger than the largest stone in Europe without being so remarkable for size as another stone in England.

Malham Cove.—A fine example of the limestone scenery of the Craven Fault. The river Aire gushes forth from the base of the cove, which can easily be seen in the same excursion as *Gordale Scar*. The nearest town is Skipton-in-Craven and the nearest station Bell Busk, but Settle is very little farther and will generally be found the most convenient starting-point.

Mardale Green, at the head of Hawes Water, is a delightful and little visited spot. In the way of climbing it commands *High Street, Harter Fell, Froswick, Ill Bell,* and *Rainsborrow Crag*. The best near climbs are about *Bleawater* and *Riggindale*.

Mellbreak.—One of the few Cumberland fells which the indefatigable Colonel Barrow seems to have left unvisited; yet no one who stops at Scale Hill or Buttermere will consider wasted a day spent upon it. The proper course is to begin at the end which faces Loweswater village and ascend by *Frier's Gill*, a nice little climb. Having reached the top of the gill and then the summit plateau, proceed to the hollow about the middle of the mountain, and from there descend the highly curious *Pillar Rake*, which gradually slopes down towards the foot of Crummock Water. It is not a climb, but any one who is not content with the study of mountain form can find climbing in the little gullies which ascend the rocks above the rake. Sheet 63 of the Ordnance map of Cumberland contains it.

Mickledoor Chimney, in the cliffs of Scafell, is not the easiest, but the most obvious point at which to attack them. It is conspicuous from the *Pikes,* and would probably be selected by any experienced stranger as the most vulnerable point. It was visited about the year 1869 by Mr. C. W. Dymond, who contributed to ' Prior's Guide ' the earliest and best description of it. He says that, ' leaving *Mickledoor* Ridge, you pass the fissure leading to *Broad Stand,* and continue descending steeply for two minutes, which brings you to a narrow gully in the rock, with a thread of water trickling down it over moss. This is the *cheminée* to be ascended, and there is no special difficulty in it until you are near the top. Here the gully, of which the ' chimney ' forms the lower section, is effectually blocked for some distance, and the only alternative is to climb out of it by the rock which forms the right wall, and which is about 12 ft. high, the lower six vertical and the upper a steep slant. This, which can only be scaled *à la* chimney-sweep, is exceedingly difficult, as is also the gymnastic feat of escaping to *terra firma* from the narrow shelf on which the shoulder-and-hip work lands you.' This is very clear and in the main correct, but there is another and easier exit much lower down called ' the Corner,' and there is a third exit only a few feet from the mouth of the chimney. All these are on the right hand, for the opposite bank is not only much higher and much smoother, but would lead to nothing if it were surmounted. It is not really necessary to enter the chimney at all, for the edge presented where the bank cuts the wall bounding the screes is quite assailable, and just right of it there is a point which may even be called easy; but two terrible accidents which have occurred at this spot prove the necessity of care.

Until the extraordinarily dry season of 1893 the moss-grown block at the very head of the chimney had never been climbed. It was accomplished on the 12th of September by Mr. W. H. Fowler. By standing on the shoulders of a tall man he was able to reach a slight hold and to establish himself on a rough rectangular block forming the floor of a recess big enough to hold one man. The block above it was holdless, and overhanging and loose stones were a great nuisance.

Micklefell.—The highest mountain in Yorkshire, but except on that account it possesses no special attraction. The best starting-point is the High Force Inn in Teesdale, 5 miles from Middleton. By making the round of the mountain from High Force to Appleby some very fine rock-scenery may be enjoyed.

Millstone grit.—A material which is very abundant in Yorkshire and Derbyshire. It is fairly firm, but seldom affords a climb of any sustained interest. Few kinds of rock weather into such eccentric forms, and of this propensity *Brimham Rocks* are a good example. It forms most of the ' Edges ' in Derbyshire, and generally speaking a precipice at the top of a hill is of this material, while those at the foot are of limestone.

Moses' Sledgate is a curious track, which has evidently been engineered with considerable care, running from near Seatoller in Borrowdale at the back of *Brandreth*, round the head of Ennerdale below *Green* and *Great Gable*, and then over Beck Head and down Gavel Neese into Wastdale. The question is, who made it and for what purpose was it used ?   A few years ago, the writer, while climbing with two friends among the crags on the Ennerdale side of *Great Gable*, stumbled quite by chance on something which seemed to throw a side-light on the question.   This was a ruined hut thickly overgrown with moss, and showing no trace of any wood having been employed in its construction.   The spot had evidently been chosen primarily with a view to concealment, and the result of enquiries kindly made since then by one of my friends has been to elicit proof of certain traditions still lingering among the older inhabitants of these dales concerning a noted distiller of illicit spirits, who flourished and defied the law among these wild retreats.   At the same time it is not easy to believe that a smuggler would have undertaken the construction of such a path as this.   In the South of England, it is true that the smugglers were considerable roadmakers ; but that was at a time when smuggling was a great and well-organised institution, and it seems much more probable in this case that Moses made use of an old path constructed for some purpose which had at that time been abandoned.

The terms ' Moses' Path ' and ' Moses' Trod ' are also used to describe this track.   It is not noticed in the guide-books, but something is said about it by Mrs. Lynn Linton.

Moss Gill, on Scafell, is the next gully on the east or *Mickledoor* side of *Steep Gill*.   The name *Sweep Gill* (' from the probable profession of the future first climber of its extraordinary vertical chimneys ') was suggested for it by Mr.

Gilson shortly after its discovery, but that name has been entirely superseded. The first mention of it in the Wastdale Head book is a note by the present writer in June 1889,

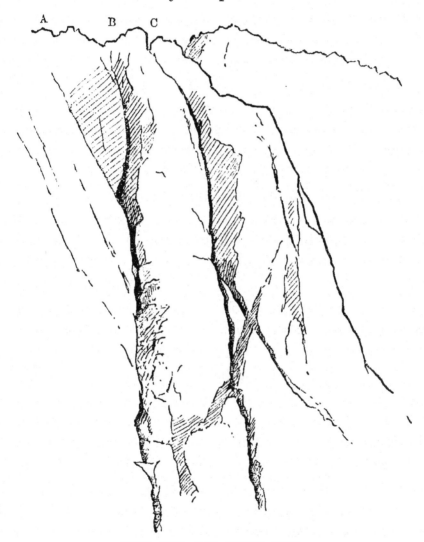

MOSS GILL AND STEEP GILL

A, *Moss Gill* (Collie's exit) ; B, *Moss Gill* (Collier's exit) ; C, Top of *Steep Gill*. Just below the point to which A and B converge is the artificial step.

recommending it to any one in search of a new and difficult climb. His party on that occasion was repulsed after reaching the great blocks, which have only been passed since by the aid of the artificial step subsequently cut in the rock. It was tried again a fortnight later by a party under Mr. R. C. Gilson, which got very nearly, but not quite as far. Two days later the same party explored the gill from above and descended in it for a considerable distance. It was not, however, till three and a half years later, at Christmas, 1892, that the climb was accomplished by Dr. J. N. Collie, G. Hastings, and J. W. Robinson, and their account of it is :

'The chief points in this climb are, First—to begin on the rock wall to the right of the foot of the gill and not in the very foot of the chimney itself, then enter the gill just below the first great pitch, which may be turned by climbing the wall on the right hand on to a grass ledge of considerable size, called the " *Tennis Court* "; enter the gill from here again, and pass into the cavern under the great boulder.'

'We found,' says Dr. Collie, 'that below the great slab which formed the roof, another smaller one was jammed in the gully, which, stretching across from side to side, formed the top of a great doorway. Under this we passed and clambered up on to the top of it. Over our heads the great rock roof stretched some distance over the gill. Our only chance was to traverse straight out along the side of the gill, till one was no longer overshadowed by the roof above, and then, if possible, climb up the face of rock and traverse back again above the obstacle into the gill once more. This was easier to plan than to carry out; absolutely no hand-hold, and only one little projecting ledge jutting out about a quarter of an inch and about two inches long to stand on, and six or eight feet of the rock wall to be traversed. I was asked to try it. Accordingly, with great deliberation, I stretched out my foot and placed the edge of my toe on the ledge. Just as I was going to put my weight on to it, off slipped my toe, and if Hastings had not quickly jerked me back, I should instantly have been dangling on the end of the rope. But we were determined not to be beaten. Hastings' ice-axe was next brought into requisition, and what followed I have no doubt will be severely criticised by more orthodox mountaineers than ourselves. As it was my suggestion I must take the blame. *Peccavi! I hacked a step in the rock*—and it was very hard work. But I should not advise any one to try and do the same thing with an ordinary axe. Hastings' axe is an extraordinary one, and was none the worse for the experiment. I then stepped across the *mauvais pas*, clambered up the rock till I had reached a spot where a capital hitch could be got over a jutting piece of rock, and the rest of the party followed. We then climbed out of the gill on the left, up some interesting slabs of rock. A few days later the gill was again ascended by a party led by Mr. J. Collier. They did not follow our track to the left after the overhanging rock had been passed, but climbed straight up, using a crack which looks impossible from down below, thus adding an extra piece of splendid climbing to the expedition.'

Only four days after Dr. Collie, a party of five climbers, led by Dr. J. Collier, made the second ascent of Moss Gill.

The description given by their precursors was of great assistance, and except that the gill was entered much lower, the
same line was followed up to the traverse from the great
boulder.   Here, instead of climbing out to the sky line on the
left side, the ascent of the gill itself was completed by climbing the vertical moss-grown wall on the right.   This part
was entirely new, and Dr. Collier's note of his variation, or
we may say correction, for his climb is the more direct of
the two, is that the ascent of the wall was made by using the
cleft of the gill for about 15 ft., when a resting place was
reached.   Above this point they climbed about 15 ft., and
then traversed out on the face of the wall for about 8 ft. by
some ledges which afforded just sufficient hold.   They then
ascended vertically about 6 or 8 ft., re-entering the cleft
above a small platform of jammed stones ('Sentry Box').
This gave a starting-point for the completion of the ascent,
which was made by climbing out on to the face of the wall to
enable the jammed stones at the top of the pitch to be turned.
These last stones did not appear to be secure and were
avoided.   From this point the gill continues upward at an
easy slope, with one pitch of about 15 ft. to the back of the
small summit on the left of *Deep Gill*.   Two days later the
ascent was repeated by Dr. Collier in company with Professor H. B. Dixon and the late Professor A. M. Marshall,
the latter of whom inserted in the Climbers' book a remarkably bold and effective outline sketch of the gill, with
explanatory notes.   Speaking of the climb, he said that Mr.
Collier led throughout, and that the success of the climb was
due entirely to him.   The climb is a very fine one, and,

except for the leader, is entirely free from danger. At the very awkward return from Tennis Court Ledge into the gully, the leader can by a short traverse fix himself directly above the rest of the party. During the traverse from the 'window' the leader can fix the rope over the 'belaying-pin.' In the great chimney the *Sentry Box* is a place of absolute safety. The climb is difficult, but no part of the chimney is harder than the short rock face leading up to Tennis Court Ledge, and the most awkward traverse (if covered with snow) is the one from Tennis Court Ledge back into the gully. For a party of three 80 ft. of rope would be enough ; 100 ft. perhaps better. On January 9, 1893, Mr. O. G. Jones attacked this formidable climb entirely by himself, following Mr. Collier's route up to the foot of the Great Chimney, and then Mr. Hastings' exit to the left. Heavy snow had fallen since the previous ascents and the climb appeared to be exceedingly difficult. Almost every hold had to be cleared of snow ; essential precautions rendered the climb of five hours' duration, and it was not completed till after dark (5.45 p.m.). While clearing snow from the more remote portions of the *Collie traverse* from the *window*, in search of the third step, the difficulty of balancing proved too great, and he fell into the gully below. A rope had been secured round the *window* and thus prevented his passing beyond the snow patch on which he fell. The *window* ' sill,' already loose, was on the verge of falling, and was therefore pushed over into the gully. Returning two days later, he found that the two lowest chimneys in the gill could be taken straight up, and that the simplest way of reaching Tennis Court

Ledge is by ' backing up ' the chimney till the level of the recess in the right-hand face is reached. ' The recess is near enough to be taken with a stride. It would seem that the Tennis Court Ledge and traverse back into the gully may be entirely dispensed with by continuing up the chimney, the small jammed stones being firm enough to render the necessary assistance. While making these suggestions concerning small details in the climb, it may be mentioned that at the *Collie traverse*, which the writer's experience leads him to think is the most dangerous piece in the gill, an axe may be of much help to a party. A man fixed on the *window sill* may press the point of the axe into a conveniently placed notch in the slab facing him, so that the lower end of the handle shall supply a firm hand-hold for any one stretching round the third step.

Heights calculated by Mr. Jones.

Foot of Gill on Rake's Progress	2,625 ft.
Snow Patch below Tennis Court Ledge . .	2,805 „
Tennis Court Ledge	2,840 „
Foot of jammed stone pitch . . .	2,870 „
Window in jammed stones	2,895 „
Snow patch above	2,920 „
Top of left-hand exit	3,140 „
Top of Moss Gill proper	3,170 „

It must, however, be borne in mind that these measurements, though useful for the purposes of comparison, cannot be absolutely correct, seeing that Scafell itself is only 3,162 ft. high. On February 11 Messrs. Slingsby, Woolley, and R. Williams found the gully very difficult owing to ice, and recorded an emphatic protest against any one following their example by attempting it, ' except when the rocks are dry and quite free from ice.'

On the last day of March Messrs. Brunskill and Gibbs followed, with a slight improvement, Dr. Collier's route, and made the subjoined observations, taken apparently with greater care than those by Mr. Jones:

Foot of Gill at Rake's Progress . . .	2,570 ft.
Snow Patch above jammed stones . . .	2,865 „
Top of Great Chimney or Moss wall . .	2,965 „
Top of Gill (neck leading to Deep Gill Pisgah)	3,065 „

It will be seen that while the points are all made lower than Mr. Jones's table, the height between the commencement of the climb and the snow patch above the jammed stones is exactly the same—295 ft. In this case an observation was taken at the cairn on the top of Scafell, and the aneroid stood at almost exactly the correct figure, which somewhat confirms the figures now given.

Napes.—A collection of fine rocks, starting up like a stack of organ pipes on the south side of *Great Gable.* The extremity of them nearest to *Kirkfell* is called *White Napes,* and sometimes Gable Horn. East of this is a gap known as *Little Hell Gate.* East of this comes *Great Napes,* and east of them again is *Great Hell Gate,* which is called Deep Gill in the Ordnance map.

In September, 1884, a note by the present writer in the book at Wastdale Head drew attention to these excellent rocks. They are now one of the most favourite climbs in

Wastdale, and contain the well-known *Needle*, the *Bear Rock*, and the *Arrowhead*, with their respective gullies and *arêtes*.

Just west of *Hell Gate* there is a considerable width of very large and steep rock, which continues nearly to the *Needle Ridge*, with only a few steep and shallow gullies, in which the grass is very rotten. West of this ridge there is a deep gully, grassy, but exceedingly steep. The ridge beyond this was ascended in April, 1892, by Messrs. Slingsby, Baker, Solly, and Brigg, who called it the *Eagle's Nest* (q.v.). The narrow gully west of this ridge is apparently that which was climbed on December 29, 1890, by Mr. R. C. Gilson. He describes it as ' the gully on the left as you face the mountain of the gully coming down left of the *Needle.*' He proceeds to say that it presented no special difficulty, except at a point about one-third of the way up, where there was a large boulder and a smooth slab thinly glazed with ice. It was claimed as a first ascent when climbed on April 17, 1892, by Messrs. Solly and Schintz. West again of this is the ridge of the *Arrowhead* (q.v.). We are here getting near the end of *Great Napes*, which are separated on the west from *White Napes* by the scree gully which is called *Little Hell Gate.*

Napes Needle.—A rock of very striking form, which, by an eminent mountaineer, has been compared to a violon-cello.

It stands at the foot of the *Needle Ridge* in the *Napes*, and was first climbed by the writer about the end of June, 1886. The second ascent was made on March 17, 1889, by Mr.

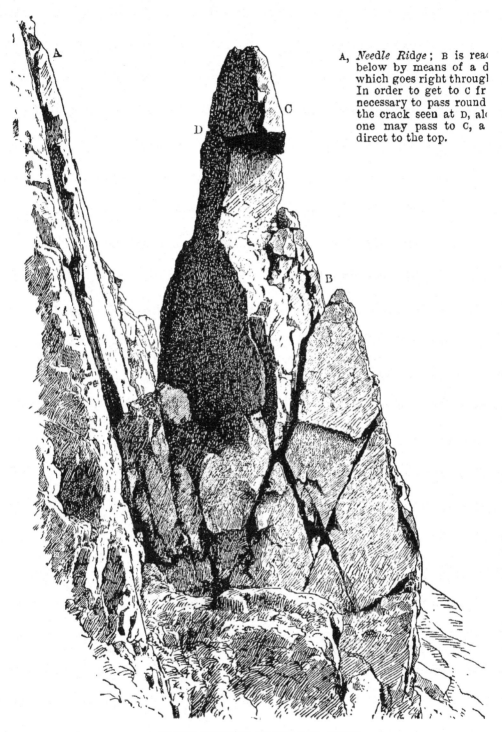

NAPES NEEDLE FROM THE WEST

G. Hastings, and the third by Mr. F. Wellford on June 22, Mr. J. W. Robinson following on August 12 in the same year.

Miss Koecher (March 31, 1890) was apparently the first lady to ascend.

It was first climbed from the west; the way on the opposite side is perhaps less severe, but longer and more varied.

The rock is frequently photographed, and an illustrated article on it appeared in the *Pall Mall Budget* of June 5, 1890.

Needle Ridge is that ridge of the *Napes* on *Great Gable* which is immediately behind the *Napes Needle*. It was discovered in 1884 by the writer and Mr. Robinson, and ascended by them in a somewhat desultory fashion ; that is to say, they cut in from the east side nearly at the top of the difficult face which forms its lower extremity, and also avoided the topmost piece by passing over on to the easy terrace on the west side of the ridge. The *arête* was climbed in a strict and conscientious manner for the first time by the writer in 1886. This was a descent, and apparently the first strict ascent was made by Messrs. Slingsby, Hastings Hopkinson, and a brother of the writer.

North Climb.—The first to describe this climb on Scafell was Mr. Seatree, who says :

' From the ridge we traversed a ledge of grass-covered rock [the Rake's Progress] to the right, until we reached a detached boulder, stepping upon which we were enabled to get hand-hold of a crevice 6 or 7 ft. from where we stood. To draw ourselves up so as to get our feet upon this was the difficulty; there is only one small foot-hold in that distance, and to have slipped here would have precipitated the climber many feet below. Having succeeded in gaining this foot-hold, we found ourselves in a small rectangular recess, with barely room to turn round. From here it was necessary to draw ourselves carefully over two other ledges into a small rift in the rocks, and then traverse on our hands and knees another narrow ledge of about 8 ft. to the left, which brought us nearly in a line with Mickledoor Ridge. From here all was comparatively smooth sailing.'

This climb had been made many years before (1869) by Major Ponsonby Cundill, R.E., who left his stick in the deep crack behind the ledge which Mr. Seatree traversed on his hands and knees. The stick was found in 1884 by Mr. Chas. Cookson. This ledge, by the way, should certainly be walked or at least sidled in an upright attitude, otherwise ungainly gambollings are necessary when the time comes for stepping off at the other end. The descent of the *North Climb* is decidedly difficult, unless the ascent has been made just previously, and the climb whether up or down is an excellent test of style.

A couple of yards to the left there is an alternative to the 'rectangular recess,' and it is known as the ' Rift.' It is to be done by a wild struggle. It was at one time the wetter and harder of the two ways, but the conditions are now reversed.

H

Old Wall.—On the east side of the Pillar Rock a natural line of rock runs down to the head of *Walker's Gully,* having, however, a narrow passage by means of which sheep may reach the Low Man. A hundred years ago or more, the shepherds built a wall of loose stones to stop the sheep, and though little of the wall remains, the name clings to the spot. At one time the *North-east Route* was usually spoken of as the *Old Wall Way.*

Patriarch.—By this name the Rev. James Jackson, of Sandwith in Cumberland, was very widely known. It is an abbreviation of one which he himself invented and assumed— 'Patriarch of the Pillarites.' Some considerable mention of him is made by Mr. Williamson, but his readers will be glad to have further particulars, for this was a man of no ordinary stamp. Born at Millom just before the series of naval victories which closed the eighteenth century, he passed his boyhood in the thick of the Buonaparte struggle and shared in it personally when a mere lad. However, he soon changed the colour of his coat and entered the Church; but long before his connection with the Pillar he had ceased to take any active part in his profession. Thenceforward he lived at his ease, amusing himself by rambles and scrambles far and near among the fells. 'I have knocked about,' he said himself, ' among the mountains ever since, till I may almost say "I knaw iv'ry craag." ' That he was somewhat of an egotist cannot be denied. In his letters as in his poems his own feats form the burden of his song. To this point all topics converged with the same certainty that all roads are said to lead to Rome. He was never tired of relating how, for instance, in his sixty-ninth year he had one day walked 46 miles in 14½ hours, on the third day following 56 miles in 18 hours, and after a similar interval 60 miles in less than 20 hours, thus accomplishing within one week three walks, any one of which might well knock up many a man of half his age ; how, on another occasion, he had found two brethren of his own cloth struggling feebly to surmount the difficulties of Rossett Gill; how, taking pity upon their tender years, he had transferred their knapsacks to his own venerable shoulders and, striding on before, encouraged them to complete their weary task. A man aged between sixty and seventy might fairly plume himself on such an exploit. He also rejoiced greatly in the fact that he had been the first student of St. Bees College—a distinction of which, as he justly said, no one could ever deprive him. But the feat on which he especially prided himself was one of bodily activity. During the third part of a century he held the living of Rivington, near Bolton-le-Moors. It chanced that the weathercock of his church had become loose, and the masons rather shrank from the risk of going up to secure it. Here was an opportunity which our friend could not forego ; and Rivington witnessed the unwonted spectacle of a beneficed clergyman of the Church of England solemnly swarming up his own steeple and making fast the vane ' under circumstances of terror which made the workmen recoil from the task, and the gazing rustics turn sick with horror at the sight ! ' While walking proudly back to his parsonage

H 2

he composed a commemorative epigram which will bear
quotation :

> Who has not heard of Steeple Jack,
>   That lion-hearted Saxon?
> Though I'm not he, he was my sire,
>   For I am 'Steeple Jackson'!

Indeed, his fancy was as lively as his limbs were supple.
He was ever on the watch for some analogy or antithesis;
ever producing some new alliteration or epigram expressive
of such contrasts as that between his age and his activity.
His favourite description of himself was ' senex juvenilis '—
an idea which he frequently put into English, e.g. :

> If this in your mind you will fix
>   When I make the Pillar my toy,
> I was born in 1, 7, 9, 6,
>   And you'll think me a nimble old boy.

On the late Mr. Maitland, a well-known climber, as only
second to himself in age and ardour, he bestowed the title
' Maitland of Many Mounts ' and ' Patriarch Presumptive of
the Pillarites.'   There is nothing strange in his thus designat-
ing a successor and bestowing titles of honour; for these are
matter of royal privilege, and he looked upon himself as the
Mountain Monarch and always expected climbers to attend
his mimic court and pay him homage.   But he had many a
high-flown alias besides.   When Mr. Pendlebury came under
his notice he contrasted himself with the Senior Wrangler,
rather neatly, as the ' Senior Scrambler '; after his ascent of
the Pillar he dubbed himself ' St. Jacobus Stylites '; and
many other titles are introduced into the occasional poems
on which he expended much of his ingenuity.

His bodily powers were not allowed to rust away. ' My adopted motto,' he said, ' is " Stare nescio," ' and some idea of his boundless love of enterprise may be formed from one of his letters : ' I have been twelve months afloat on the wide, wide sea. I have been beneath the falls of Niagara. I have sung " God save the King " in the hall of St. Peter's ; I have ascended Vesuvius in the eruption of 1828 ; I have capped Snowdon in Wales and Slieve Donard in Ireland, and nearly all the hills in this district. . . . It only remains for me to mount the Pillar Rock ! ' Before the end of the following May this hope was gratified, and a proud moment it was for this veteran climber when, seated serenely on the summit, he was able to record in a Greek inscription (written, as he carefully notes, ' without specs ') his ascent of the famous rock. Think of the life, the energy, the determination that must have been in him ! Years seemed to be powerless to check the current of his blood. Where are we to look for another of his age—he was now in his eightieth year—showing any approach to the same combination of enterprise, pluck and bodily vigour ? It cannot be wondered at that his success filled him with the keenest delight. He wrote off at once in high glee to his friends and felt quite injured if, in their reply or their delay in replying, he detected any sign of indifference to his exploit. But true to his motto ' Stare nescio,' he was not content with this. Within a month we find him expressing a fear that his title ' Patriarch of the Pillarites ' might not be acknowledged by ' the Western division of the Order,' and announcing his intention of climbing the Pillar from the west also in order to secure his claim. He playfully proposes, moreover, that while he, 'the aged errant knight,' with his faithful squire toiled up from the west, a certain fair Pillarite should arrive at the summit from the east and crown his success on the spot by the bestowal on him of her hand and heart. According to all approved precedent the 'aged errant knight' ought to have bound his lady's favour around his clerical hat and ranged the mountains extorting from the passing tourist at the point of his alpenstock a confession of her peerless beauty; or for her sake betaken himself to the Rock and there passed nights of vigil and days of toil assisting distressed damsels in the terrible passage of the 'Slab.' Whatever he did, he made no attempt on the west route. Perhaps despair of the reward had cooled his zeal—zeal conditional like that of the Hindoo teacher who, when asked whether he professed the creed which he was anxious to teach, naïvely replied, 'I am not a Christian; but I expect to be one shortly—if sufficient inducement offers.'

There is a sad and sharp contrast in turning from his high spirits and playful fancy to his sudden death. It has been described elsewhere. Though fourscore and two was (as he himself expressed it on the very day of his death) the 'howdah' on his back, it cannot be said that the ever-growing howdah had crushed its bearer. His vigour was unimpaired. Like Walter Ewbank,

> To the very last,
> He had the lightest foot in Ennerdale.

Indeed, the same thing might have happened to a boy. It was an accident; but it might be rash to say that it was a misfortune, or that he would himself have regarded any other death as preferable. His life had already been longer and more varied than falls to ordinary men; but the change could not long have been delayed. A few months would have seen his faculties failing and his powers decayed. To a man of his habits and temperament inaction would have been the most terrible affliction, and though he might have dragged on for years, his strength would truly have been labour and sorrow.

Two years before he had stood close to this very spot. 'Almost all the mountains,' he said, 'which I had known in youth, in manhood, and in old age were visible, and seemed to give me a kindly greeting " for auld lang syne." In the fervour of admiration I might have chanted, " Nunc dimittis, Domine, servum tuum in pace." ' We may well believe that, had the old man foreseen his fate, he would have gladly welcomed it, and have found for it no fitter place among all his beloved mountains than this quiet cove almost within the shadow of the majestic rock.

Patterdale is a place where a climber may spend a week or two with much enjoyment, though the quality of the rocks is by no means first-rate. It is the best centre for *Helvellyn*, *Fairfield*, and *St. Sunday Crag*, and convenient for *Swarthbeck* and the whole *High Street* range. On *Place Fell*, fine as it looks, there is not much worth climbing. *Deepdale* and *Dovedale* are both worth exploring.

Pavey Ark, one of the Langdale Pikes, is easily reached in three-quarters of an hour from Dungeon Gill. On it will be found some splendid climbing, including the *Big Gully*, the *Little Gully*, *Jack's Rake* (q.v.), and many minor points of interest. The two chief gullies stand on either side of a buttress of rock, the top of which forms a tooth on the sky line. The *Little Gully* is on the south side of it, and is V-shaped, giving a very straightforward but pleasant climb. But the *Great Gully* has two considerable difficulties, one low down and the other near the top. The lower is caused by a huge block covering a considerable cavern. The way is either right through the cavern and out again through a narrow hole, or up a high grassy bank on the right hand. In either case a narrow place is reached, walled in between the big block and a smaller one on the right hand. Here the difficulty is that the walls nearly meet towards the top, so that it is necessary, in order to get room for the head, to go rather 'outside.' However, a second man with a rope can hold the leader very securely, and a piece of rock having come away, the headroom is much more commodious than it used to be. Just below the level of *Jack's Rake* there are some very 'brant and slape' inclines of wet or muddy rock, which most people consider the worst part of the climb. There is very little hold, and what there is was on the occasion of the first ascent lubricated by a film of fine mud. On reaching *Jack's Rake* several variations may be made, and straight ahead there is a very neat little chimney. These upper rocks are of splendid gripping quality; rough as a cow's tongue, it would be quite difficult to make a slip on them. The Big Gully was climbed by the writer in the summer of 1882, and the small one in June 1886. In March 1887 Mr.

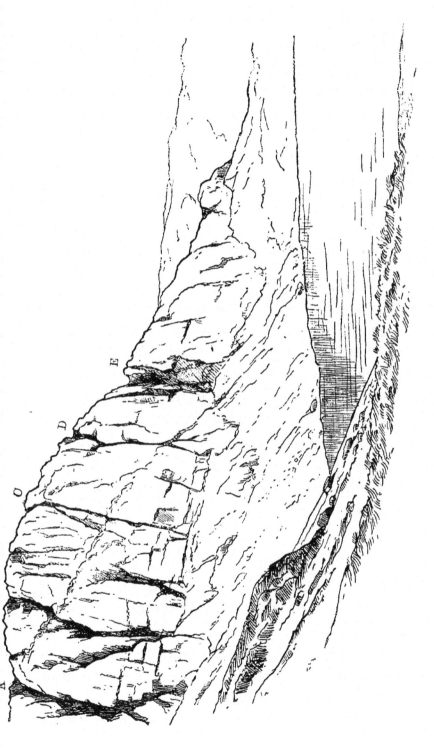

PAVEY ARK (NEAR VIEW)

A, Narrow gully; B, Big gully; C, D, Smaller gullies; E, Wide scree gully.
From the foot of E to A runs *Jack's Rake*.

Slingsby made a note about the former in the Wastdale Head book. He says that it took his party two hours and forty minutes, but his estimate of the height of the gully at 1,300 ft. is more than double of the truth, and must be due to a slip of the pen.

In the book at Millbeck there is a note by the same distinguished climber, dated May 30, 1887, in which he records an ascent of this gully made by Miss Mabel Hastings, and gives the height of it as 600 or 650 ft.

Penyghent.—The sixth in height of the Yorkshire hills, but long supposed, on account of its finer shape, to be the highest of them all. As late as 1770 it was reckoned at 3,930 ft. It can be ascended from Horton station in little over an hour. Celtic scholars revel in the name; they practically agree that it means 'head of something,' but cannot accept each other's views as to what that something is. When Defoe was in this neighbourhood he saw 'nothing but high mountains, which had a terrible aspect, and more frightful than any in Monmouthshire or Derbyshire, especially *Pengent Hill*.'

Piers Gill, in Wastdale, on the north front of *Lingmell*, has a vast literature of its own. As a rock ravine, not in limestone, it is only second to *Deep Gill* on *Scafell* and the great gully in the Wastwater *Screes*, both of which are far less easy of access than this, which can be reached from Wastdale Head in half an hour. The difficulties depend entirely on the quantity of water. One, the 'cave pitch,' may be passed at the cost of a wetting almost at any time;

but above it is another, known as the 'Bridge Fall,' from a vast column of fallen rock which spans the stream a few yards above it, which is at all times difficult, and in nineteen seasons out of twenty wholly impossible.

Until the unprecedented drought of 1893 it had never been climbed. Even then a less brilliant climber than Dr. Collier would scarcely have succeeded. His ascent was made on April 29, 1893, and his companions were Messrs. Winser, W. Jones, and Fairbairn. The big pitch was found to be 40 or 50 ft. high, the lowest part of it apparently overhanging. The first few feet were climbed about three feet to the right of the falling water, after which the leader was able to reach the other side of the gill by stretching his left foot across it just outside the water. By this means this great and hitherto insuperable difficulty was overcome. Unless we are entering on a cycle of dry seasons, the exploit is one which will not be repeated for some time.

Various accidents and minor mishaps have taken place in Piers Gill. One is described by Mr. Payn, and the injured man was, I believe, a shepherd called Tom Hale. Mr. W. O. Burrows had a bad fall above the bridge, and people descending from the *Pikes* are often pounded about the same spot. Some years ago a tourist had to pass the night in the gill without food, but protested that he was 'quite consoled by the beautiful scenery.' The discovery of the route up the east side of the *Pillar Rock* was within an ace of being delayed for years, owing to the band of bold explorers who were to work it out becoming entangled in *Piers Gill* while on their way to *Wastdale Head.*

The name is spelt ' Pease ' by Mr. Payn and by most of the early authorities, and judging by the analogy of other places in the North of England this would appear to be more correct.

Pike o' Stickle, also known as *Steel Pike* and sometimes as the *Sugarloaf,* drops into Langdale from the north in one continuous slope, which for length and steepness has not many rivals in England. The top piece of the hill is curiously symmetrical, and resembles a haycock or a thimble. It is not easy to find satisfactory climbs on it. Mr. Gwynne says of it : ' A very fine peak, that, viewed from the valley, has very much the appearance of the Mönch. It runs down towards the *Stake* Pass in a spur, which must be the starting-point of most of the climbs on this mountain. There is a curious gully here, too, which is worthy of the climber's attention. It does not run from top to bottom, but suddenly begins about the middle of the crag. The difficulty is to get at this gully, and some pretty climbing can be obtained in the attempt.'

Pillar Rock. —There are but three directions from which the *Pillar* is commonly approached—namely, Ennerdale (Gillerthwaite), Buttermere, and Wastdale Head. In each case the guide-books (except Baddeley's) exhibit a suspicious shyness of specifying any time for the walk. Wherever the present writer gives times, they must be understood to be the quickest of which he happens to have made any note ; for the best test of times is a ' reductio ad minima.' A journey may be indefinitely prolonged, but it cannot be shortened beyond a certain limit; thus, *Scafell Pike* cannot be reached from Wastdale Head in much less than 60 minutes of hard going, while the walk up the Pillar Fell cannot be cut down much below 75 minutes. This supplies us with a trustworthy comparison, although for a hot day that pace is not to be

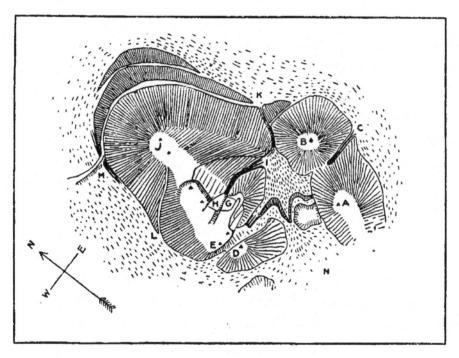

PILLAR ROCK

A, B, Summits of Shamrock; C, Shamrock gully; D, Pisgah; E, High Man; G, Curtain; H, Steep Grass; I, Foot of Great Chimney; I, K, Walker's gully; J, Low Man; L, J, West route; M, Waterfall; N, I, East Scree.

recommended; in each case double the time is not more than a fair allowance. Never let yourself be hurried at starting, come home as hard as ever you like; it is the chamois-hunter's system, and by far the best. Baddeley seems to reverse the principle, for he allows 2 to $2\frac{1}{2}$ hours for the ascent viâ Black Sail, and says that it is shorter by Wind Gap ; yet for the *descent* from Wind Gap (which is, say, 20 minutes short of the summit) he gives as a fair allowance

PILLAR ROCK FROM THE NORTH

A, *High Man* ; B, *Low Man* ; C, *Shamrock* ; D, *Walker's gully* ; E, Below this is the *waterfall*.

The *terrace* runs past the foot of Walker's gully to the foot of the *waterfall*.

2 to 3 hours. Perhaps he preferred conforming to what is apparently the approved fox-hunting style :

> Harkaway ! See, she's off ! O'er hill and through whol
> We spank till we're gaily nar done,
> Than, hingan a lip like a motherless fwol,
> *Sledder heàmmward, but nit in a run.*'

From Ennerdale: From Gillerthwaite, a farmhouse nearly a mile and a half above the lake, the Pillar is not far distant;

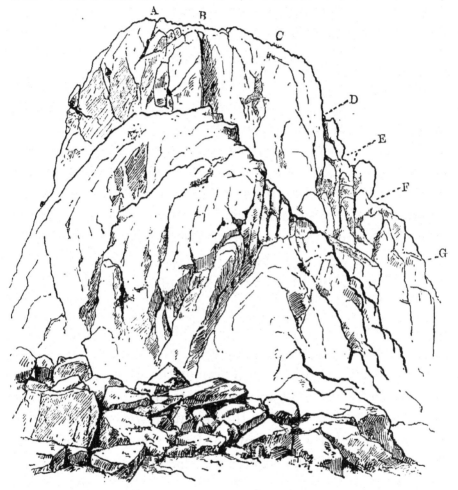

PILLAR ROCK FROM THE SOUTH

A, Top of rock and of *West Jordan climb* ; B, Top of *Central Jordan climb* ; C, Top of *East Jordan climb* ; D, G, The *Curtain* ; E, The *Notch* ; F, The *Ledge*. The mass of rock in the foreground is *Pisgah*.

but the direct way is exceedingly rough, and it will be found best to make use of the path up *Wingate Cove*, skirting round the mountain, when by that means a considerable height has been gained. The way is so rough that many people think it an economy of labour to go right on up the gap, and then left over the summit of the mountain.

One of the best ways of approaching the Pillar is to sleep at the little inn at the foot of the lake and row up from there to the water head. For walking the whole way from the inn to the fell-top Baddeley allows 3 to 3½ hours.

From Buttermere : After crossing *Scarf Gap* some keep to the track as far as the summit of the Black Sail Pass, and then turn to the right up the ridge of the Pillar Fell, while others adopt the more laborious plan of working upwards after descending the valley until nearly opposite the Rock, which in this way is certainly seen to much greater advantage. If the return be made by way of the mountain ridge, some little time may be saved by descending into Ennerdale down *Green Cove*, nearly half a mile short of Black Sail and 250 ft. higher; for Black Sail, being much nearer the head of the valley than either Scarf Gap or the Pillar, can only be used for going from one to the other at the expense of making a considerable *détour*. For the ascent, however, Green Cove is not so decidedly recommended, as many will prefer to make the round by the regular pass for the sake of the more gradual rise.

From Wastdale : The vast majority of visitors come from this direction, and almost all follow the same track, plodding up from Mosedale to the top of *Black Sail* and then turning left along the ridge of the mountain. Mosedale, by the way, must not be confused with any of the numerous other valleys

of the same name: it sometimes appears in the form 'Mores-
dale' or 'Mossdale' (Moos-thal, near Laibach in Austria, is
exactly parallel), and generally indicates scenery of a dreary
character; for such valleys are often, as in this case, the
half-drained beds of ancient lakes, by the loss of which the
scenery has seriously suffered.

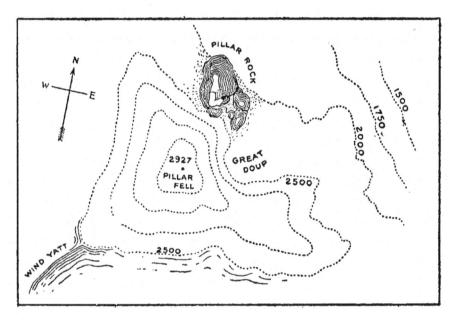

PILLAR FELL

Ladies who ascend by Black Sail will find it best to keep
to the path as long as possible, i.e. as far as the top of the
pass, but others may save something by breasting the hill on
the left soon after reaching *Gatherstone Head*, apparently
a glacier mound, which rises just beyond where the track
crosses the stream (Gatherstone Beck) which comes down
from the pass.

On reaching the ridge it is no doubt safer, especially if there be mist about, for those who are not familiar with the way to go right on to the flat top of the mountain ; the proper point from which to commence the descent is easily found, in all weathers, by following the compass-needle from the cairn to the edge of the mountain ; a rough and steep descent of 400 ft. follows, which in winter demands considerable care. At first the course is to the right, but it soon strikes a small ridge which curves down to the Rock. It is, however, a waste of labour to ascend to the summit of the mountain at all. The ridge of the mountain is divided into steps, and at the foot of the uppermost of these a deep cove called *Great Doup* is seen on the right. It may be recognised even in a mist, as it is just beyond a curious rock running out with a narrow edged top many feet from the hill-side. Less than 100 yards down the Doup the falling scree has nearly buried the cairn and iron cross erected to the memory of the Rev. James Jackson. Beyond this, as soon as the big rocks on the left permit, the track skirts round, and after one or two ups and downs comes into full view of the famous Rock. If, however, the object be to reach the north or lowest side of the Rock, it is not necessary to descend into Ennerdale from Black Sail ; for there is the *High Level*, a fine scramble all along the breast of the mountain from *Green Cove*—the first large hollow on the right, just beyond *Lookingsteads* ; but the way is rather intricate, and unless properly hit off involves considerable fatigue and loss of time. At the very least half an hour will be required in either direction, and a stranger will certainly take much longer.

Those who are anxious to pursue ' t' bainest rwoad ' may save ten minutes or more in the walk from Wastdale by making use of *Wind Gap* at the head of Mosedale. Hard work it undeniably is, but more shady than Black Sail, and —when the way is familiar, though no one can go very far wrong, unless he clings to the main valley too long and goes up to *Blackem* (Black Combe) *Head*—quicker also, occupying about ninety minutes. Mr. James Payn calls it (poetically) ' a sort of perpendicular shaft—a chimney such as no sweep would adventure, but would use the machine—which is said to be the dalesman's pass into Ennerdale ; you may thank your stars that it is not *your* pass.'

It really adds little to the labour of this way and affords a far finer walk if the complete circuit of Mosedale be made along the hill-tops. Ascending behind the inn and keeping round just under *Stirrup Crag*—the north end of *Yewbarrow*, *Dore Head* is soon reached, and it is easy walking by the *Chair, Red Pike, Black Crag* and *Wind Gap* on to the *Pillar Fell.*

For the return to Wastdale *Wind Gap* is very rough and hardly to be recommended. Mr. Baddeley is not very con- sistent about it, for he says, ' the best descent is by *Windy Gap* '; but again, ' the descent from *Windy Gap* to Wastdale is, for reasons stated before, unsatisfactory '; and thereupon he recommends Black Sail. The latter gives a rapid descent —the inn may be reached in twenty-five minutes from the top of the pass ; but a quicker return may be made by crossing the ridge after emerging from Great Doup, and shooting down *Wistow Crags* into Mosedale by a large gully filled with deliciously fine scree.

Should it be preferred to make the circuit of Mosedale on the return journey, an equally fine glissade may be enjoyed

PILLAR ROCK FROM THE WEST

A, Summit of *High Man* ; B, *Pisgah* ; C, *Low Man* ; D, *Jordan Gap.*
The *West route* ascends from this side to the depression between A and C.

from *Dore Head* ; but the screes require judicious selection and dexterity on the part of the slider.

It may here be said that stout walkers may visit all the

mountains of Wastdale Head in one day comfortably, and in few places is a finer walk to be found. Start, say, at 10 A.M. for Scafell; then, by Mickledoor, the Pike, Great End, Sty Head, Great Gable and Kirkfell to the Pillar, returning in the manner described above in time for dinner. In June 1864, as Ritson's Visitors' Book records, J. M. Elliott, of Trin. Coll. Camb., made this round, including Steeple and Yewbarrow, and found that it took eight and a half hours; probably, however, he came over Stirrup Crag and not Yewbarrow *top*, which would entail something like three miles extra walking. He approached Scafell by way of Mickledoor, returning from it to the same point, and those who do not know the Broad Stand well had better follow his example; for it is a bit of a climb, and the descent especially is not easy to find. By going to Mickledoor first (and there is no shorter way to Scafell) each man can see what he has before him, and decide for himself whether it would not be better to leave Scafell out of his programme.

Before entering into the history of the Pillar it is almost indispensable to give a short general description of its main features in order to assist the comprehension of the facts narrated. Difficult as it must always be to find an image which shall supply a stranger with any clear idea of a mass so irregular and unsymmetrical as this, yet its general appearance and the arrangement of its parts may be roughly apprehended in the following manner :—Imagine a large two-gabled church planted on the side of a steep hill. From the western and loftier gable let there rise, at the end nearest the mountain, a stunted tower. Finally let the building be shattered and all but overwhelmed under an avalanche of *débris*. What will be the effect? Naturally the stream of stones will be much deeper above than below, and, while nearly burying the tower and upper ends of the roof, will flow along between the two gables and run off, as rainwater would do, at the far end. Angular fragments, however, remain at rest unless the slope is very steep, and consequently a long talus will be formed sloping down to the brink of the sudden drop at an angle of something like 45 degrees. Here we have a fair representation of the Pillar mass: the tower will be the High Man, and the gable from which it rises the Low Man. It will be readily understood that the second gable may be a source of some confusion to those who are ignorant that there is more than one, and from some points may disguise or altogether conceal the tower. This is why it is called the *Sham Rock*; but it is only from below that it would be recognised as part of the Pillar mass, for from above it is wholly insignificant. When viewed from immediately below, the tower is concealed behind the gable from which it rises, and the whole mass of rock bears a rough resemblance to the letter M ; but from above, the High Man, with which alone the climber from the east side has to reckon, is also the only part of the rock which he is likely to observe. The result is that, when the Low Man is mentioned to anyone who knows only the Easy Way, the reply is usually on the model of the poet Words-worth's only joke : ' Why, my good man, till this moment I was not even aware that there *was* a Low Man ! ' Yet the Low Man is by far the finer object of the two, and its cliffs are at least six times as high as those of what is called the High Man. The only side from which the latter shows a respectable elevation is the west, where the scree lies much lower, because it has a free escape, instead of being pent up between the two gables like the east scree.

In winter-time, when the inequalities are all smoothed over with a sheet of hard snow, both sides of the rock are rather dangerous, but especially the eastern, where a man who slipped would have the greatest difficulty in stopping himself before he shot over the precipitous gully at the end. This gully (occupying, as it were, the place of the water-pipe) is known, in allusion to an accident which occurred there in 1883, as *Walker's Gully.*

When the question arises of how to climb the *High Man*, it is obvious that the scree just above it will be the nearest point to the summit; but equally obvious that the climb, though short, would be nearly vertical. The plan which at once suggests itself for getting to the top is to work round to the back of the rock and climb it from the top of the ridge behind. The ridge may be reached from either side, and in this fact we have the secret of two of the most important climbs.

So much for the general appearance of the Pillar; but the part which admits of the easiest and most varied attack is the east wall of the *High Man*, and of this side it is necessary to give a more detailed description. This part of the rock is the only one which is at all well known to the general public, and its chief features, being well marked, have for the most part received, by common consent of

climbers, distinctive names. In order to see the formation
of the rock properly it is well worth the climber's while to
descend for a few yards and mount the *Sham Rock* on the
other side of the east scree. The peculiar structure of the
opposite wall may now be clearly seen.

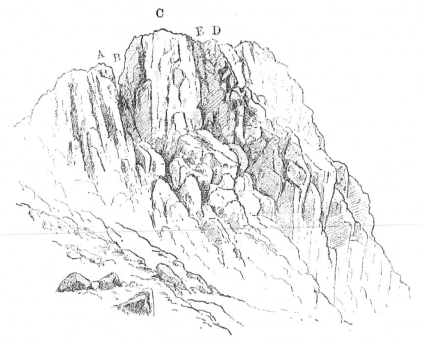

PILLAR ROCK FROM THE SOUTH-EAST
A, *Pisgah*; B, *Jordan*; C, Summit; D, Top of *Curtain*; E, Corner between the
Curtain and the main rock.

On our left hand, between the mountain and the rock, is
seen an outlying mass severed from the High Man by a deep
square-cut gap. When the Pillar is looked at from the
direction of the mountain-top, this gap is entirely concealed
by the outlying piece, which then appears to present a fairly
easy way direct to the summit. 'The climber (says Mr.

Williamson) mounts gaily and with confidence, only to find himself cut off from the High Man by an impassable cleft.' He sees it indeed with his eyes, but he cannot go up thither. Hence the names—P*isgah* for the false rock, and *Jordan* for the chasm. A very well-known Pillarite once proposed to bridge the cleft with a plank or ladder and hold a tea-party on the top. This very original idea was not carried into execution, but certainly, without some such application, the passage of *Jordan Gap* is a formidable undertaking; for the north wall is only less vertical than the other, and though barely 60 ft. high—not much more, that is, than half as much as must be climbed by any other route—this is decidedly one of those cases in which the longer way round will prove to be the shorter way up.

On the extreme right—and rather below us—is the nearly level top of the Low Man; while not far from where broken cliffs lead up to the higher rock a curious natural post standing on the ridge marks the point from which a small deep channel is seen to come down towards *Walker's Gully.* This channel is of small importance, except that high up on the southern bank of it the glacier markings are most distinctly to be seen. The channel itself soon curves more towards the north and plunges over the fearful cliff which faces the Liza, forming the key to the great climb on that face. From the foot of *Jordan Gap* a broad smooth slope of rock runs horizontally along the face of the High Man, giving to it somewhat the formation of the ' pent-house wall ' of a tennis court. The steepness of the scree, which runs down from left to right before our feet, makes the drop from this slope much greater at the Low Man end; but it will give no false idea of this side to say that, roughly speaking, the cliff is broken into three fairly equal portions, of about 60 ft. each, namely, a vertical wall above, connected with a steep and rugged part below by a smooth stretch sloping at an angle not far short of 40 degrees. The importance of this 'pent-house' is very great; for, as it gives an easy passage right across this face of the rock, every climb which is possible from below may be cut into from the side, and thus more than half the labour of the ascent is saved. Indeed, any mountain which allows its entire front to be traversed in this way by a passable ledge exposes every weak point in so reckless a manner that the attack becomes marvellously simplified.

Lastly should be noticed two rough curtains of rock which run down from the top of the Stone near the centre, and enclose between them what is called the *Great Chimney*. This chimney is the key to the climb on this side. The curtain on the south of it is the only one which is at all complete, and as it forms a kind of *arête* running up to the summit, it is known indifferently by either name—the *Curtain* or the *Arête*.

The easiest way to picture to oneself the features of the Great Chimney is to imagine a huge armchair, the 'seat' of which measures 20 yards from back to front and is tipped uncomfortably forward and downward at an angle of nearly 45 degrees. The *Curtain* forms the right 'arm,' and from a level with the top of the 'back,' which is 50 ft. high, runs down very nearly but not quite as far as the front edge of the

' seat.' In the narrow space thus left lies the *Ledge*, which makes it possible to pass round under the end of the arm and gain the ' seat,' which is called the *Steep Grass*. The same point may also be reached by climbing, as an alternative to the *Ledge*, over the lower part of the ' arm ' through a deep nick—the *Notch* ; and in either case the joint between ' arm ' and ' back,' being badly cracked, offers an easy way (the ' small chimney ' or ' jammed-stone chimney ') of reaching the top of the back, which is the edge of a small plateau forming the summit of the High Man. Lastly, it should be noticed that the *Steep Grass* can only be reached from below by a severe climb of 70 ft.—the *Great Chimney* climb.

The side from which the Pillar is commonly climbed is not that by which the summit was first attained. The first successful attempt was made from the West, and it is doubtful whether for a quarter of a century any other route was known. But on the discovery of the Easy Way the older route was forgotten, and now enjoys a reputation for difficulty which is not deserved : it is looked upon as some little distinction to have accomplished it. In the preface to one of Wordsworth's poems the year 1826 is mentioned as the date of the first ascent. This is confirmed by a comparison of the second and third editions of Otley's ' Guide ' (1825 and 1827), in the former of which the rock is declared unclimbable, while the latter mentions the victory of ' an adventurous shepherd.' The successful climber was not, however, a shepherd, but a cooper, named Atkinson, and living at Croftfoot, in Ennerdale. It is likely that his adventurous soul may have been fired by Otley's declaration that the rock was inaccessible. The perseverance of a friend has hunted out a contemporary notice of the ascent in the county paper, which remarks that, ' though the undertaking has been attempted by *thousands*, it was always relinquished as hopeless.' This proves, at all events, that even then the rock had a reputation. Subjoined is a list of those who have followed on Atkinson's track, so far as is known, up to 1873 :

J. Colebank (shepherd) ;
W. Tyson (shepherd), and J. Braithwaite (shepherd) ;
Lieut. Wilson, R.N. ;
C. A. O. Baumgartner ;
M. Beachcroft and C. Tucker.

Summarising the various methods of ascending the rock, we may say that the west side first yielded in 1826 ; the east side probably about 1860 ; the south side in 1882, and the north side in 1891. The *Easy Way* (as it is generally called) on the east side was discovered in 1863 by a party of Cambridge men led by Mr. Conybeare, and Mr. A. J. Butler, the late editor of the *Alpine Journal*. Mr. Leslie Stephen had visited the rock earlier in that year without finding a way up it, but in 1865 he was more successful, and wrote an account of it in Ritson's book ; the account, as usual, was first defaced and afterwards stolen. The *North-east*, or *Old Wall*, *way* was discovered by Matthew Barnes, the Keswick guide, while with Mr. Graves, of Manchester. The central and western climbs from *Jordan* were done by the writer in 1882, as was the eastern one in 1884, the last being scarcely justifiable under any circumstances, and especially without a rope. The direct climb of the *Great Chimney* (starting on the south wall of it) was done about the same time, and curiously enough—for it is safe and comparatively easy—does not appear to have been done since. The long climb on the north face was accomplished by Messrs. Hastings, Slingsby, and the writer in 1891. It has been described in an illustrated article in *Black and White* (June 4, 1892), and by Mr. Gwynne in the *Pall Mall Budget*. It should not be touched except by experienced climbers.

Pinnacle Bield, on the east side of *Glaramara*, is a rocky part of the mountain and a famous stronghold for foxes. On the way up from *Langstrath* there is a very steep bit for about 500 ft.

Pisgah.—A name given in 1882 to the outlying rock on the south side of the Pillar Rock, from which it is severed by an all but impassable chasm, not seen until it bars the way. The term has in subsequent years been applied almost generically.

Pitch : any sudden drop in the course of a rock gully, usually caused by some large stone choking the channel and penning back the loose stones behind it. Such a stone is then said to be 'jammed,' 'wedged,' or 'pitched,' and is sometimes called a 'chockstone' (q.v.).

Pot-holes are frequent in the Yorkshire limestone. The rivers for considerable distances have underground courses. At each spot where the roof of one of these tunnels happens to fall in a 'pot-hole' is produced. They are very numerous about Settle and Clapham. Some are of very great depth and can only be explored with the aid of much cordage and many lights. The explorer of pot-holes has to face all the perils of severe rock climbing, and, moreover, to face them for the most part in the dark. It would be hard to imagine anything more weird than one of these darksome journeys, rendered doubly impressive by the roar of unseen waters and the knowledge that abrupt pitches of vast depth are apt to occur in the course of the channel without the slightest warning. (See *Alum Pot, Dunald Mill Hole, Gaping Gill Hole*.)

Pow : a sluggish rivulet.

Professor's Chimney.—A name bestowed by Messrs. Hopkinson on the exit most towards the left hand as one comes up *Deep Gill* on *Scafell*. Out of this chimney, again to the left, diverges that which leads up to the neck between the *Scafell Pillar* and its Pisgah. To this latter chimney the name is erroneously applied by many, though, indeed, they might urge with some reason that if it comes to a scramble for one name between two gullies the more frequented ought to get it.

Rainsborrow Crag.—A noble rock in Kentdale, West-morland. It is, perhaps, most easily got at from Staveley, but from Ambleside it is only necessary to cross the Garbourne Pass, and the crag is at once conspicuous. It is of the same type as *Froswick* and *Ill Bell*, but finer and more sheer than either of them.

Rake : a word common in Derbyshire, Yorkshire, and the Lakes, which has been much misunderstood. It usually happens to be a scree-gully, but the fundamental idea is straightness.

Rake's Progress.—This is a natural gallery on the face of the Mickledoor crags of *Scafell*. It has been best described by Mr. Williamson, who says : '*Mickledoor* may be reached by scrambling up the steeply sloping screes which form its Wastdale slope ; but the easier and more romantic approach is by the grassy ledge, which will be seen projecting from the face of the Scafell precipice. This ledge or shelf is in but few places less than four feet wide. In places it is composed of shattered heaps of rock, which seem barely to keep their equilibrium ; but though there is a precipice of considerable height on the left hand, the passage along the ledge is free from risk so long as the rock wall on the right is closely hugged. By one who watched from below the passage along the ledge of some of the early pioneers of lake climbing it was christened the *Rake's Progress*, and the name appears apt when it is remembered that the ledge leads from the lower limb of the *Lord's Rake* to the *Mickledoor Ridge*.' The first published description of the *Rake's Progress* is contained in a letter by the late Mr. Maitland to one of the local papers in October 1881. He there states that he had recently traversed it for the fifth time, but had not previously to that occasion visited Deep Gill. Several grand climbs start from the *Progress*, including *North Climb, Collier's Climb, Moss Gill, Steep Gill*, and the *Scafell Pillar*.

Raven Crag.—This name is generally the sign of a hard, if not of a good, climb. One of the finest stands on the west side of Thirlmere, near the foot, or what used to be the foot of it before Manchester took it in hand ; a second is on the *Pillar Fell* just east of the rock ; a third and fourth on *Brandreth* and *Gable*, and indeed there is one on almost every fell.

Red Pike, in Cumberland, overlooking Buttermere, is a syenite hill, and commands a glorious view, especially strong in lakes, but there is next to no climbing to be had on it. The best way up it is to follow the course of Ruddy Beck from the southernmost corner of Crummock Water, but the rocky amphitheatre in which Bleaberry Tarn lies is better seen if the somewhat rougher route by Sourmilkgill and its east bank be followed.

Red Pike, also in Cumberland, is a Wastdale fell, and lies between *Yewbarrow* and the *Steeple*. The north side of it has abundance of small climbs, which, with the exception of *Yewbarrow*, are, perhaps, more easily reached than any others from the inn at Wastdale Head ; but they are little visited, because everyone wants to fly at the highest game and do the climbs which are most talked about. This fell is sometimes called *Chair*, from the fact of there being a curious stone seat on it near the ridge, and not far from *Door Head.*

Red Screes, in Westmorland (2,541 ft.), are very steep in the direction of the Kirkstone (after which the pass of that name is said to be called), falling about 1,000 ft. in a horizontal distance of a quarter of a mile; but the ascent is not more than an exhilarating scramble. There is a well-known view from the top.

Rope.—Some remarks on the use of the rope as a safeguard in climbing will be found in the Introduction.

Rossett Gill.—A rough pass just over 2,000 ft. in height, which is the only approach from Langdale to Scafell, Gable, and the Wastdale fells generally. On the Langdale side you cannot go far wrong, but it is very rugged, so rugged that Mr. Payn has caustically observed that all expeditions in this region admit of being made by driving, by riding, or by walking, 'except Rossett Gill, which must be done on all fours.' On the Eskhause side the walking is perfectly easy, but mistakes are very liable to occur. On this high ground mists are extremely frequent, and blinding rain is abundant. The result is that people making for Langdale are surprised at having to mount again after the long descent to Angle Tarn, and often end by going away to the left down Langstrath, and find themselves to their great surprise in Borrowdale. The only safeguard is, of course, to bear clearly in mind that the ups and downs hereabout are considerable, and to arm oneself with map and compass.

Saddleback (2,847 ft.) was at one time thought to be higher than its neighbour Skiddaw. To Mrs. Radcliffe, on the summit of the latter in 1795, the former was 'now preeminent over Skiddaw.' 'The Beauties of England' informs

K

us that ' the views from the summit are exceedingly exten-
sive, but those immediately under the eye on the mountain
itself so tremendous and appalling that few persons have
sufficient resolution to experience the emotions which those
awful scenes inspire.' We have a very full account of an
ascent made in 1793. The narrator says : 'When we had
ascended about a mile, one of the party, on looking round,
was so astonished with the different appearance of objects in
the valley so far beneath us that he declined proceeding.
We had not gone much further till the other companion (of
the relator) was suddenly taken ill and wished to loose blood
and return.'

The great feature of the mountain is its southern front,
which is cut away to form enormous cloughs, divided by
narrow ridges. The latter are the Edges of Saddleback.
Narrow Edge (as *Halls Fell top* is now generally called) is
the finest and most romantic. It runs up from Threlkeld,
where there is a convenient station. The proper name of
Broad Edge is *Gategill Fell*. Part of *Middle Tongue*
straight behind the lead-mine is also very narrow. A writer
in the *Penny Magazine* for 1837 speaks of ' the ' serrated
precipices above Threlkeld,' and adds, ' One of these is called
Razor Edge.' That name, however, has now for many
years at least been used as the equivalent of *Sharp Edge*,
which is on the east side of the mountain and on the north
side of *Scales Tarn*, and at one time enjoyed a tremendous
reputation as a perilous climb.

The name of the mountain itself has been jeered at as a
post-boy's name, and romantically-minded people use the

name Blencathara, for which many Celtic etymons have been suggested. The most usual form seems to have been Blenkarthur, and only the more northern of the two peaks was so called.

The quickest ascent of the mountain is from Threlkeld up *Narrow Edge*, but if the return is to Keswick, it should be made along the shoulder towards Skiddaw, and so by Brundholme Wood.

Sail.—This word, in the opinion of Dr. Murray, the learned editor of the new 'English Dictionary,' signifies ' a soaring dome-shaped summit.' It occurs as a hill-name in the Grassmoor group, near Buttermere in Cumberland; but the characteristics required by the above definition are, to say the least, not conspicuously evident either there or in the other cases where this element is found in fell-country place-names. (See *Black Sail*.)

St. Bees.—In Cumberland, on the west coast. Several accidents have occurred on the cliffs here. They are of sandstone, and incline to be rotten. The best are about *Fleswick Bay*. The height is only about 200 ft. The Rev. James Jackson—the Patriarch (q.v.)—lived at Sandwith close by, and was fond of climbing about on these cliffs.

St. John's Vale.—A name of modern invention, which has ousted *Buresdale* (q.v.). It is used in an article in the *Gentleman's Magazine* for 1754, and also in 'Gray's Journal,' which possibly misled Sir Walter Scott, whose poem caused it to meet with general acceptance.

St. Sunday Crag, in Westmorland (sheet 19 of the Ord-nance map), is of far more importance than *Helvellyn* to the views of and from Ullswater. Moreover, it has some capital crags facing north-west, among which many a good rock-problem may be found. They were long a favourite scrambling-ground with Major Cundill, R.E., the inventor of the *North Climb* on *Scafell*, and are within easy reach of Patterdale.

Scafell (3,162 ft.) presents some fine rocks to Eskdale, but the grandest rocks, both to look at and to climb, are towards *Mickledoor*. As a climbing-ground it is perhaps even more popular than the *Pillar*, especially in winter. In consequence of this the ground has been gone over very closely by climbers of exceptional skill, and climbing of a somewhat desperate character has occasionally been indulged in. This applies mainly to the west side of Mickledoor. The other side is easier, and has long been more or less well known.

Mr. Green says of it: 'The crags on the south-west [of Mickledoor], though seeming frightfully to oppose all passage, have been ascended as the readiest way to the top of Scafell, and, amongst other adventurers, by Mr. Thomas Tyson, of Wastdale Head, and Mr. Towers, of Toes [in Eskdale]; but Messrs. Ottley and Birkett contented themselves by proceed-ing for some distance in the direction of Eskdale, to a deep fissure, through which they scrambled to the top of Scafell.'

It might be thought that this 'fissure' was 'Mickledoor

Chimney,' but it is more likely that it was another and easier gully a good way farther down.

Mr. Herman Prior's excellent ' Pedestrian Guide' (3rd edition, p. 194) has a very clear and accurate account of it from the pen of Mr. C. W. Dymond, who visited it about 1869, and another in Mr. C. N. Williamson's second article

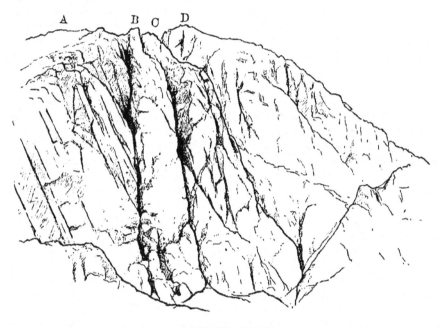

SCAFELL CRAGS

A, Top of *Broad Stand*; B, *Pisgah*; C, *Scafell Pillar*; D, Head of *Deep Gill*.

in *All the Year Round* for November 8, 1884; and in the local press scores of descriptions have appeared.

The beginning of the climb is very easily overlooked by a stranger, being just a vertical slit about eighteen inches wide, by means of which it is easy to walk three or four yards straight into the mountain. It will be found by descending

the Eskdale slope from Mickledoor ridge for twenty-one
yards, and disregarding a much more promising point which
presents itself midway and is noticed both by Professor
Tyndall and Mr. Dymond. The floor of the proper ' adit '
rises slightly towards the inner end, and consequently allows

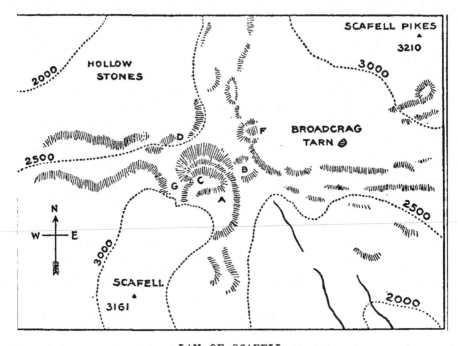

LAN OF SCAFELL

A, *Broad Stand*; B, *Mickledoor Ridge*; C, *Scafell Pillar*; D, *Lord's Rake*;
F, *Pikes Crag*; G, *Deep Gill.*

an easy exit to be made on the left-hand side. From this
point three large steps in the rock, each 7 ft. to 10 ft. high
have to be mounted, and many will be reminded of the
ascent of the Great Pyramid. What builders call the ' riser '
of each step is vertical, but the ' tread ' of the two upper ones
becomes very steep and smooth, and when there is ice about

it, this is the chief danger of the climb. If a fall took place it would probably be to the left hand, in which direction the rock is much planed away, and forms a steep and continuous slope almost to the foot of the Mickledoor Chimney.

This slope is climbable, but far from easy. At the top of the steps the Broad Stand proper begins, at the head of which there is one little bit to climb, and then a walk among huge blocks of stone leads out on to the ridge of Scafell, close to the head of Deep Gill.

The way is not easy to miss, but in descending—especially in misty weather—mistakes are often made, either in finding the entrance at the top or the steps at the bottom. The latter difficulty is the more serious, but may be obviated by keeping close to the foot of the cliff on the left hand and making straight for Mickledoor ridge; when further progress is barred, the exit is reached by a short descent to the right.

Scafell Pikes—the highest mountain in England (3,210 ft.). Curiously enough the name seems to be very modern. Till quite the end of last century it was always known as ' The Pikes,' and it was only when careful surveys promoted it that it became necessary to add the name of its finer-shaped and better-known neighbour, to show what ' Pikes ' were being spoken of. The present name, there- fore, and the older form, ' Pikes of Scafell,' really mean ' The Pikes near Scafell.'

On the Eskdale side there are a few climbs, including *Doe Crag*; but the best are on the side of *Great End* and *Lingmell*, which are merely buttresses of it.

Scafell Pillar stands between *Deep Gill* and *Steep Gill*. It has a short side close to the summit ridge of *Scafell*, and

SCAFELL PILLAR (SEEN ACROSS DEEP GILL)

a long side towards the *Rake's Progress.* The first ascent was made on the short side by the writer on September 3,

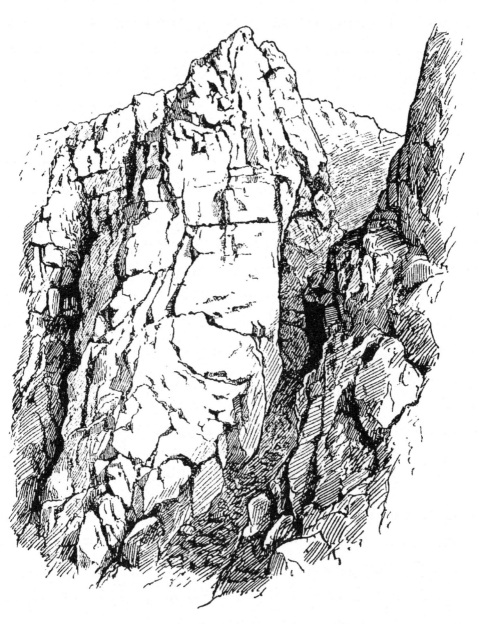

SCAFELL PILLAR AND THE UPPER PITCH OF DEEP GILL

1884, and the first from the Rake's Progress by Mr. Robinson and the writer on the 20th of the same month.

They climbed by way of *Steep Gill* on to the Low Man, and thence to the High Man. On July 15, 1888, a way was made up the outside of the rock from near the foot of *Steep Gill* by Messrs. Slingsby, Hastings, E. Hopkinson, and the writer. Miss Corder made the first lady's ascent by the short way (August 1887), and Miss M. Watson the first by the outside route (June 1890), both ladies having the advantage of Mr. Robinson's escort.   Marvellous feats of climbing and engineering have been performed by the brothers Hopkinson in their endeavours to make a way direct into *Deep Gill*, in which they have not entirely succeeded.

Scree : the *débris* of decaying rocks, forming a talus on the lower parts of a mountain.   It is the Icelandic ' skrida.'

Screes (The).— A long range flanking Wastwater on the south-west. They are often called the ' Wastdale' Screes, but it appears from Hutchinson that they were in his time known as the ' Eskdale' Screes, and—like most hills at that period—were said to be a mile high. Apparently in those days they thought less of the climbs on it than of the sheep-runs, which latter are in Eskdale. The rock is of very loose construction and comes away at a touch, or without one, sometimes many tons at a time ; but it improves towards the foot of the lake, and the great bastion opposite Wastdale Hall is full of magnificent climbing. The writer, at the suggestion of Mr. G. Musgrave, tried the great gully both alone and in good company, namely, that of two of the party

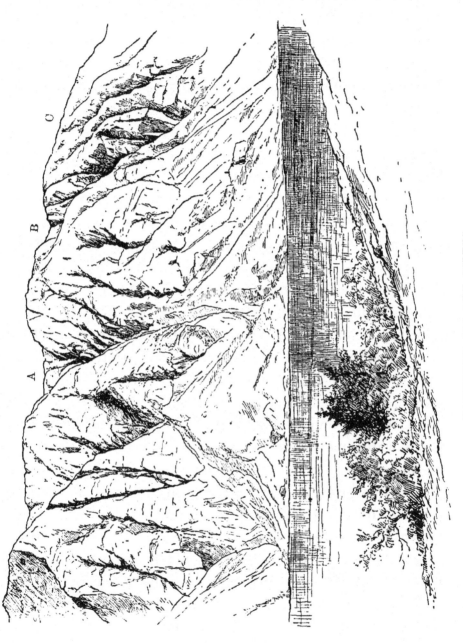

WASTWATER AND THE SCREES

which ultimately succeeded.   Dr. Collie contributed a vivid account of the first ascent to the *Scottish Mountaineering Journal,* a publication which should be better known to climbers.   The party found no difficulty till they were in the left-hand branch above the point where the gully divides, and the first pitch gave them some trouble, as the stream, being frozen, formed a cascade of ice, and they were forced on to the buttress which divides the two gullies.   'Hastings was sent on to prospect, whilst I had to back him up as far as possible.   With considerable trouble he managed to traverse back to the left into the main gully, using in-finitesimal knobs of rock for hand and foot hold.   We then followed him, and found ourselves in a narrow cleft cut far into the side of the hill.   Perpendicular walls rose on either side for several hundred feet; above us stretched cascade after cascade of solid ice, always at a very steep angle, and sometimes perpendicular.   Up these we cut our way with our axes, sometimes being helped by making the steps close to the walls on either side, and using any small inequalities on the rock-face to steady us in our steps.   At last we came to the final pitch.   Far up above at the top, the stream coming over an overhanging ledge on the right had frozen into masses of insecure icicles, some being 20 ft. to 30 ft. long.   Obviously we could not climb up these. However, at the left-hand corner at the top of the pitch a rock was wedged, which overhung, leaving underneath a cave of considerable size.   We managed to get as far up as the cave, in which we placed Robinson, where he hitched himself to a jammed boulder at the back.   I was placed in a somewhat insecure position ; my right foot occupied a capacious hole cut in the bottom of the icicles, whilst my left was far away on the other side of the gully on a small, but obliging, shelf in the rock-face. In this interesting attitude, like the Colossus of Rhodes, I spanned the gulf, and was anchored both to the boulder and to Robinson as well. Then Hastings, with considerable agility, climbed on to my shoulders. From that exalted position he could reach the edge of the overhanging stone underneath which Robinson was shivering, and was thus enabled to pull himself up on to the top. Robinson and I afterwards ascended this formidable place by means of the moral support of the rope alone. But I know that in my case, if that moral support had not been capable of standing the strain produced by a dead weight of about ten stone, I should probably have been spoiling a patch of snow several hundreds of feet lower down the gill. Above this pitch the climbing is easier as the gully opens out.'

Sergeant Crag.—About half a mile up the valley of Longstrath, which bounds Glaramara on the east as Borrow-dale does on the west, there is a line of crag on the left hand. The part nearest to Eagle Crag is called Sergeant Crag, and is some 300 ft. higher than the other, which is Bull Crag.

In these rocks there is a very fine gully, discovered in 1886 by Mr. Robinson and the writer, for whom a high wet slab of smooth slate proved too difficult. In September last the former returned to the attack accompanied by Mr. O. G.

Jones, who, taking a different and to all appearance more difficult way to the right, forced his way over the two stones which form the pitch. His companion followed by working out of the gill to the right and in again above the obstacle, and this way has commended itself to later climbers.

'There are six large pitches and several small ones. The total climb must be 500 ft., and the climbing is of exceptional interest all the way.'

Shamrock, in Cumberland, stands just east of the *Pillar Rock*, divided from it only by *Walker's Gully*.

Seen from *Scarf Gap* it looks very well, and its outline can with difficulty be distinguished from that of the main rock. It derives its name (bestowed on it about 1882) from this deceptive character. The face of it towards the north affords a good climb, and on the east side there is a gully, which is choked near the top by a block, which makes one of the stiffest pitches in all Cumberland. It was first climbed, with the aid of deep snow, by a party led by Messrs. Hastings and E. Haskett Smith in March 1887, and in December 1890 Mr. Hastings succeeded in repeating his ascent without any snowdrift to help him, as did Dr. Collier exactly two years later.

Sharp Edge, on Saddleback, runs along the north side of Scales Tarn. Mr. Prior's 'Guide' observes: 'The ascent (or descent) by this Edge is considered something of an exploit, but without sufficient reason. To a giddy head, indeed, it is unquestionably several degrees worse than Striding Edge, which it somewhat resembles; possibly, to a head so constituted, just without the limits of safety, as Striding Edge is decidedly well within them. The main difficulty lies in the descent of the cliff above the " Edge," and in the two or three rocky knolls by which this cliff connects itself with the latter, and from which there is an unpleasant drop on each side. . . . Excepting *head*, however, no other quality of a cragsman is required for Sharp Edge; the footing is ample, and the hands would be less called into requisition than even on Striding Edge.'

This is a very just estimate, but it need hardly be said that not only Sharp Edge but also those on the Threlkeld side undergo marvellous changes in winter, and then give splendid chances of real mountaineering practice.

Shuttenoer is mentioned by more than one of the old authorities as one of the rocks at Lowdore between which the water falls. My belief is that the intelligent travellers of that date, not having mastered the ' Cummerlan' mak o' toak,' mistook for the name of the rock what was merely intended for a casual description of it, namely, ' Shuttan' ower '—' shooting over,' ' projecting.'

Sike : a rill in marshy ground.

Silver Howe (1,345 ft.), near Grasmere, is only notable as being the scene of the annual fell race, or ' Guides' race,' as it is sometimes called, though there are few guides, and of them very few would have any chance of success in this race. The course is uphill to a flag and down again. The time is generally about ten minutes to go up and something less than five minutes to come down. It is a pretty race to watch, but the scientific interest for mountaineers would be increased if the course were free from all obstacles and of accurately measured height and length.

Skew Gill.—A curious deep channel in the Wastdale side of Great End, giving a convenient approach to the foot of the gullies on the other side. To go by Grainy Gill and this one, and so up Cust's Gully, has for many years been the regulation expedition for the first day of a winter sojourn at Wastdale Head.

Skiddaw (Cumberland, sh. 56) is 3,058 ft. high, ' with two heads like unto *Parnassus*,' as old Camden observed, and Wordsworth and others have repeated it after him. On this characteristic, which is not very strongly marked, many derivations of the name have been based. In older writings, however, the word much more commonly ends in -*ow*, a termination which in countless instances represents the well-known word ' how.' Whatever its name may signify, Skiddaw is not a mountaineer's mountain, and no amount of snow and ice can make it so. As a local bard has truly sung :

> Laal brag it is for any man
>   To clim oop Skidder side ;
> Auld wives and barns on Jackasses
>   To tippy twop ma ride.

It is true that there are great facilities for procuring ginger-beer on the way, but even that luxury is scarcely an adequate compensation for the complete absence of anything like a respectable rock on the mountain. Keswick has Skiddaw

almost entirely to itself, and on the matter of routes it will
be enough to say that by the back of Latrigg and the
gingerbeer shanties is the easiest way, and by Millbeck and
Carlside is the shortest and quickest, being made up of two
miles of good road and of two of steep fell as against five
miles of easy hillside.

The mountain used to enjoy a great reputation, and is put
first in Camden's ' Byword ' :

> Skiddaw, Lauvellin and Casticand
> Are the highest hills in all England,

and the early climbers of it were deeply impressed with the
importance of their adventurous undertaking.

Mrs. Radcliffe, in 1795, ascended ' this tremendous mountain,' and says that when they were still more than a mile
from the summit ' the air now became very thin,' and ' the
way was indeed dreadfully sublime.' On reaching the top
they ' stood on a pinnacle commanding the whole dome of
the sky,' but unluckily ' the German Ocean was so far off as
to be discernible only like a mist.'

Even Hutchinson remarks that, on the top, ' the air was
remarkably sharp and thin compared with that of the valley,
and respiration seemed to be performed with a kind of
oppression.'

Skiddaw reserves what little natural ferocity it has for
Dead Crags on the north side, but there are also a few rocky
bits on the side which faces Bassenthwaite Water.

Smoking Rock is at the head of *Great Doup*, east
of the *Pillar Stone* and level with the ridge of the *Pillar*

Fell. For fear of the name being adduced as a proof of recent volcanic action it is well to say that it is so called not as itself smoking, but because a well-known climber of the old school loved to smoke an evening pipe upon it.

It affords a pleasant climb taken on the outside straight up from the foot. This was done by a party of four, of whom the writer was one, on June 5, 1889. See a note in the Wastdale Head Visitors' Book at p. 250.

Somersetshire has little to attract the mountaineer, except the very remarkable limestone scenery on the south side of the Mendips at Cheddar, Ebber and Wookey. There are magnificent cliffs and pinnacles, especially at the first-named place, but not many bits of satisfactory climbing. The cliffs are rotten at one point, unclimbably vertical at another, and perhaps at a third the climber is pestered by clouds of angry jackdaws. Ebber Rocks are rather more broken, but on the whole the climbing is not worth much at either place, though the scenery both above ground and below it is such as no one ought to miss.

Stand.—See under *Broad Stand.*

Steep Gill.—On Scafell, forming the boundary of the Scafell Pillar on the Mickledoor side. It contains a very striking vertical chimney more than 50 ft. high, the upper part of which is rather a tight fit for any but the slimmest figures. At the foot of this chimney on the right-hand side there is an exit by which either the ridge of the Scafell Pillar can be reached or the chimney circumvented. The Gill becomes very wet and steep just below the top, and extreme care is necessary in following it out on to the neck between Scafell Pillar and the mountain. Except in dry weather this bit may be considered a little dangerous. It is usual and more interesting to work out here by a grass ledge on the right on to the Low Man. The Gill was discovered by the writer, and first climbed by him and Mr. Robinson in September 1884. A note by the former in the Visitors' Book at Wastdale Head describes it as ' a chimney of unusual steepness and severity.' The name is quite recent.

Steeple.—In Cumberland, separated from *Pillar Fell* by *Wind Gap*. There are some grand scrambles on the Ennerdale side of it, and it is extremely interesting to the student of mountain structure to note the points of parallelism between this group and that of *Scafell*, *Wind Gap*, of course, representing *Mickledoor*.

Stirrup Crag, on the north end of Yewbarrow, is probably the very nearest climb to Wastdale Head, and may therefore be useful in cases when a wet day clears up towards evening and exercise within easy reach is required. The quickest way to it is to cross the beck by the bridge behind the inn and go up the hill straight to the rectangular clump of larches, and then on beyond it in the same direction. There is a nice little climb on an isolated bit of rock, noted by Mr. Robinson in the Wastdale book, at Easter in 1888. The little rock should be crossed from north to south and the same course continued up to the open fell above, after which a short descent towards Door Head, keeping rather to the left hand, will bring to light several small but pretty rock-problems.

Striding Edge, a ridge on the east side of *Helvellyn*, is called in one of the old maps *Strathon Edge*. The difficulties of it have been absurdly exaggerated. Miss Braddon wrote amusingly about the exploits upon it of a certain gallant colonel, identified by Colonel Barrow with himself. In winter it is sometimes an exciting approach to *Helvellyn*, in summer just a pleasant walk. The idea of its danger probably arose from the celebrity given to the death of Charles Gough by the poems of Scott and Wordsworth.

Sty Head.—This name applies to the top only of the pass from Borrowdale to Wastdale, though often incorrectly used to designate the whole way from Seathwaite to Wastdale Head. The natives always speak of the whole pass as *The Sty* or *The Stee*. Hutchinson says, and the statement has been repeated by Lord Macaulay, that this was at one time the only road between Keswick and the West Coast. It has lately been proposed to construct a driving road across it, but the project is not likely to be carried out for some time. The way is not easy to find on a really dark night. Some years ago two tourists who had been benighted on the pass wrote a most amusing account of their experiences in the *Graphic*, and it is only a year or two since two well-known Cumberland climbers were caught in the same ignominious fashion.

Swarthbeck, in Westmorland, and on the east shore of Ullswater and the west slope of *Arthur's Pike*, would appear to be identical with the 'chasm' noticed by Mr. Radcliffe in 1795. 'Among the boldest fells that breast the lake on the left shore are *Holling Fell* and *Swarth Fell*, now no longer boasting any part of the forest of Martindale, but showing huge walls of naked rock and scars which many torrents have inflicted. One channel only in this dry season retained its shining stream. The chasm was dreadful, parting the mountain from the summit to the base.' It occurred to Messrs. T. and E. Westmorland, of Penrith, to explore it, and they found it to be a capital little climb. They published a bright and vigorous account of their climb in a Penrith paper, in consequence of which a good sprinkling of climbers have been induced to visit it. The writer has cause to remember the steepness of this gill, for on one occasion, just as the last few feet of the climb were being done, the alpen-stocks, which had been a great impediment all the way up, slipped and fell, and were afterwards found on the scree at the very bottom. The steamers stop at Howtown, about a mile further up the lake, and the inn at that place is much the most convenient place to start from.

Tarn Crag (Cumberland, sh. 57) is a precipitous bit of not very sound rock, perhaps 200 to 300 ft. in height, rising on the south-west side of Bowscale Tarn. There is a better-known crag of this name just by Scales Tarn on Saddle-back, and, in fact, they are exceedingly numerous, which is natural enough, seeing that it is essential to every genuine

tarn that it should be more or less under a precipice of
some sort.

Toe-scrape.—May be defined as ' foot-hold at or below
its minimum.'

Tors, on *Dartmoor* (q.v.).—The word is also found in
Derbyshire, though not there applied to quite the same kind
of rock.   The Ordnance also give it in some instances in
the North of England ; but there it is by no means clear that
they have taken pains to distinguish it from the sound of the
word ' haw ' when there is a final *t* in the preceding word.
What, for instance, they call Hen Tor may be in reality
Hent Haw.   In Scotland *tor* is, of course, a common com-
ponent in place names.

A few of the more interesting *tors* are—

Belliver Tor.—Turn squarely to the right two miles from
   Two Bridges on the Moreton Hampstead Road.

Blackingstone Rock.—A true tor, though not on Dartmoor.   It is a fine piece of rock two miles east of
   Moreton Hampstead.   It is of loaf-like form, and gave
   a difficult climb until a staircase of solid and obtrusive
   construction was put there.

Brent Tor.—A curious cone of volcanic rock a long mile
   south-west of Brentor Station, and fully four miles
   north of Tavistock.

Fur Tor.—About six miles in a northerly direction from
   Merivale Bridge, Two Bridges, or Princetown.

Hey Tor.—Four miles west of Bovey Tracy ; was quite
   a nice climb, but has been spoilt by artificial aids.

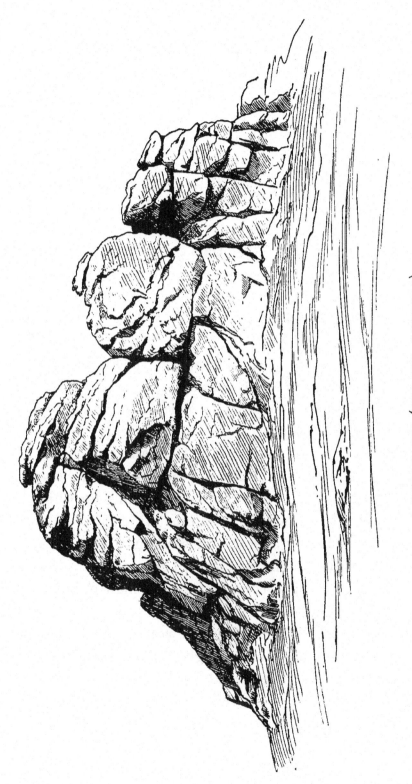

A TYPICAL TOR (HEY TOR, DARTMOOR)

Links (Great) Tor.—About two miles east of Bridestow station.

Longaford Tor.—Strike off to the left about halfway between Two Bridges and Post Bridge.

Mis Tor (Great and Little).—Two miles north from Merivale Bridge. They are fine objects, especially the larger.

Row Tor.—On the West Dart some four miles north of Two Bridges. It has a very striking block of granite on it.

Sheep's Tor.—About two miles east of Dousland Station. It is finely shaped.

Shellstone Tor.—Near Throwleigh, about halfway between Chagford and Oakhampton.

Staple Tor.—Under a mile north-west from Merivale Bridge, and four miles east of Tavistock.

Vixen Tor.—One mile from Merivale Bridge, or four miles north from Dousland Station. It is near the Walkham River, and is almost the only tor which has a distinct reputation as a climb. It is got at by means of the cleft shown in the illustration. Here it is usual to 'back up.' The struggles of generations of climbers are said to have communicated a high polish to the surface of the cleft.

Watern Tor.—Five or six miles west of Chagford, on the left bank of the North Teign. It has three towers of friable granite much weathered.

Yar Tor.—Halfway between Two Bridges and Buckland-in-the-Moor; it has a curiously fortified appearance.

VIXEN TOR (DARTMOOR)

Vixen Tor.—One of the finest of the Devonshire *Tors* (q.v.).

Walker's Gully is the precipice in which ends the East Scree, between the *Pillar Rock* and the *Shamrock*. It is named after an unfortunate youth of seventeen who was killed by falling over it on Good Friday, 1883. He had reached the rock with four companions, and found there two climbers from Bolton, who had been trying for nearly three hours to find a way up, and were apparently then standing in or near Jordan Gap. Seeing Walker, they shouted to him for advice as to the ascent. He thereupon endeavoured to join them by sliding down on the snow; but he had miscalculated the pace, and when he reached the rock at which he had aimed, it was only to find that his impetus was too powerful to be arrested. He shot off to one side, rolled over once or twice, and then darted away down the steep East Scree, passing the Bolton men, who could not see him owing to that position, and disappeared over the precipice.

Wallow Crag, a long mile south of Keswick, is abrupt but not high, and somewhat incumbered by trees. It contains *Lady's Rake,* and *Falcon Crag* is really a continuation of it. Both are too near Keswick to please climbers, who do not enjoy having their every movement watched by waggon-loads of excursionists.

Wanthwaite Crags (Cumberland, sh. 64) rise on the east side of the stream which flows, or used to flow, from Thirlmere. There is good climbing in them, and they are easily reached from Keswick (1 hour), or Grasmere, taking the Keswick coach as far as the foot of Thirlmere ; and Threlkeld station is nearer still (half an hour). The rocky part has a height of 600 to 700 ft. Bram Crag, just a little south, is really part of it.

Wastdale.—There are two valleys of this name, one near Shap in Westmorland, and the other and more famous in Cumberland, at the head of Wastwater. It is the Chamouni of England, and would be the Zermatt also, only it lacks the charm of a railway. Fine climbs abound among the various fells which hem it closely in. (See under the heads of *Scafell, Lingmell, Great Gable, Pillar, Yewbarrow, Steeple, Red Pike,* and *Great End.*) A well-filled ' Climbing book ' is kept at the inn, where also are some fine rock-views and a very complete set of large-scale maps. Men with luggage must drive up from Drigg Station ; those who have none can walk over *Burnmoor* from Boot Station in one hour and a half or less.

Westmorland, as a climber's county, is second only to Cumberland. Langdale is perhaps the pick of it, but about Patterdale, Mardale, and Kentdale abundant work may be found, and there are few parts of the whole county which have not small local climbs of good quality set in the midst of charming scenery. Defoe's account of it is extremely amusing :

' I now entered *Westmorland,* a county eminent only for being the wildest, most barren, and frightful of any that I have passed over in *England* or in *Wales.* The west side,

which borders on *Cumberland*, is indeed bounded by a chain
of almost unpassable Mountains, which in the language of
the country are called F*ells*. . . . It must be owned,
however, that here are some very pleasant manufacturing
towns.'

The notion of lake scenery being rendered tolerable by
manufacturing towns is one which may be recommended to
the Defence Society ; but Mr. Defoe has not done yet :

' When we entered at the South Part of this County, I
began indeed to think of the mountains of Snowden in North
Wales, seeing nothing round me in many places but unpassable Hills whose tops covered with snow seemed to tell us
all the pleasant part of England was at an end.'

Westmorland's Cairn is a conspicuous object at the
edge nearest to Wastwater of the summit plateau of *Great
Gable*. There is a wide-spread impression that this cairn,
which is built in a style which would do credit to a profes-
sioual ' waller,' was intended to celebrate a climb ; but
Messrs. T. and E. Westmorland, of Penrith, who built it in
July 1876, wished to mark a point from which they ' fear-
lessly assert that the detail view far surpasses any view from
Scafell Pikes, *Helvellyn*, or *Skiddaw*, or even of the whole
Lake District.' At the same time the short cliff on the edge
of which the cairn stands is full of neat ' problems,' and it is
customary to pay it a visit on the way to Gable Top after a
climb on the *Napes*.

Wetherlam, in Lancashire, is about 2,500 ft., and has
some crags on the north side among which here and there

good climbing may be found. They can be reached in about an hour and a half from either Coniston or the inn at Skelwith Bridge. In an article signed ' H. A. G.' (i.e. Gwynne), which appeared in the *Pall Mall Gazette* in April 1892, the following description of a part of it is given : ' On the west face there is a bold cliff that stands between two steep gullies. The cliff itself can be climbed, and in winter either of the gullies would afford a good hour's hard step-cutting. Just now, after the late snowstorm, the mountaineer would have the excitement of cutting through a snow-cornice when he arrives at the top. The precipice itself is fairly easy. I happened to find it in very bad condition. All the rocks were sheeted with ice and extremely dangerous. In one part there was a narrow, steep gully ending in a fall. It was full of snow and looked solid. I had scarcely put my foot on it when the snow slipped away with a hiss and left me grabbing at a knob of iced rock that luckily was small enough for my grasp. This climb, however, in ordinary weather is by no means difficult.'

Whernside, in Yorkshire, was considered even as late as 1770 to be the highest mountain in England, 4,050 ft. above the sea.

White Gill, in Langdale, Westmorland, nearly at the back of the inn at *Millbeck,* derives its chief interest from the loss of the two Greens there, so graphically described by De Quincey.

This and the other gills between it and *Stickle Tarn* afford good climbing up the walls by which they are enclosed.

Winter Climbs.—Only a few years ago a man who announced that he was going to the Lakes in the depth of winter would have been thought mad. Exclamations of this kind are even now not unfrequently called forth at that season of the year; yet they seem to have little or no effect in diminishing the number of those who year by year find themselves somehow attracted to the little inns which lie at the foot of Snowdon or of Scafell Pikes.

On Swiss mountains winter excursions have been made even by ladies, and perhaps the British public was first rendered familiar with the idea by Mrs. Burnaby's book on the subject. But, in truth, the invention is no new one, and those bold innovators who first dared to break through the pale of custom and to visit North Wales or the Lakes in mid-winter were richly repaid for their audacity; for there is hardly any time of year at which a trip to Lakeland is more thoroughly enjoyable.

In the first place, there is no crowd. You can be sure that you will get a bed, and that the people of the house will not be, as they too often are in the summer time, too much overworked to have time to make you comfortable, or too full of custom to care much whether you are comfortable or not. Out of doors there is the same delightful difference. You stride cheerily along, freed for a time from the din of toiling cities, and are not harassed at every turn by howling herds of unappreciative 'trippers.' The few who do meet on the mountains are all bent on the same errand and 'mean business'; half-hearted folk who have not quite made up their minds whether they care for the mountains or not, people who come to the Lakes for fashion's sake, or just to be able to say that they have been there, are snugly at home coddling themselves before the fire. You will have no companions but life-long lovers of the mountains, and robust young fellows whose highest ambition is to gain admission to the Alpine Club, or, having gained it, to learn to wield with some appearance of dexterity the ponderous ice-axes which are indispensable to the dignity of their position. Then what views are to be had through the clear, frosty air! How different are the firm outlines of those distant peaks from the hazy indistinctness which usually falls to the lot of the summer tourist! What sensation is more delightful than that of tramping along while the crisp snow crunches under foot, and gazing upward at the lean black crags standing boldly out from the long smooth slopes of dazzling white! There is no great variety of colour; for the rocks, though a few are reddish, are for the most part of grey in varying shades; yet there is no monotony.

It is true that January days have one fault; they are too short. Or shall we not rather say that they seem so because —like youth, like life itself—they are delightful? They would not be too short if they were passed (let us say) in breaking stones by the roadside. After all, the hills hereabouts are not so big but that in eight or nine hours of brisk exertion a very satisfactory day's work can be accomplished. In short, youth and strength (and no one can be said to have left these behind who can still derive enjoyment from a winter's day on the Fells) can hardly find a more delightful way of spending a week of fine frosty weather.

Wrynose.—The pass between Dunnerdale and Little Langdale, and the meeting-point of the three counties of Cumberland, Westmorland, and Lancashire.

It would seem that we are poorer than our ancestors by one mountain, for all the old authorities speak of this as a stupendous peak. *Defoe's Tour* (1753) says : ' Wrynose, one of its highest Hills, is remarkable for its three Shire Stones, a Foot Distance each.' The name properly understood would have put them right. The natives pronounce it 'raynus,' and I have not the least doubt that it represents 'Raven's Hause.' Indeed, in early charters the form 'Wreneshals' is actually found, and the intermediate form 'Wrenose' is found in a sixteenth-century map.

Yewbarrow (2,058 ft. ; Cumberland sh. 74) is a nar- row ridge a couple of miles long, which, seen end-on from the shore of Wastwater, has all the appearance of a sharp peak. There is climbing at the north end about *Door Head* and *Stirrup Crag*, while towards the south end there are two very interesting square-cut ' doors ' in the summit ridge, apparently due to 'intrusive dykes,' and beyond them the little climb called Bell Rib End.

Yorkshire (see *Attermire, Calf, Craven, Gordale, Ingleborough, Malham, Micklefell, Penyghent, Pot-holes, Whernside*)—a county whose uplands fall naturally into three great divisions, only one of which, however, demands the attention of the mountaineer. The chalk *Wolds* in the East Riding, and the moorland group formed by the *Hambleton* and *Cleveland Hills*, may be dismissed here with a mere mention. The third division, which constitutes a portion of the *Pennine Chain*, and, entering the county from Westmorland and Durham on the north, stretches in an unbroken line down its western border to Derbyshire on the south, approaches more nearly to the mountain standard. Even in this division, however, only that portion which lies to the north of Skipton attains to any considerable importance. It is in this latter district—in *Craven*, that is, and in the valleys of the Yore, the Swale, and the Tees—that we must look for the finest hill scenery in Yorkshire. Most of these mountains consist of limestone, capped in many cases by millstone grit, and of such summits some twenty-five or thirty rise to a height of 2,000 ft. Very few of them, however, exhibit individuality of outline, and, with the exception of the low lines of limestone precipice which occasionally girdle them, and of the wasting mill-stone bluffs which, as in the case of *Pen-hill* or *Ingleborough*, sometimes guard their highest slopes, they are altogether innocent of crag. If any climbing is to be found at all, it will probably be among the numerous 'pot-holes,' or on the limestone 'scars,' such as *Attermire* or *Gordale*, which mark the line of the Craven Fault. The *Howgill Fells*, north of Sedburgh, form an exception to the above remarks. (See *Calf.*)

Although the climber may find little opportunity to exercise his art among the Yorkshire mountains, yet the ordinary hill-lover will discover ample recompense for the time spent in an exploration of these hills and dales. The ascent of *Micklefell*, of *Great Whernside*, of *Penyghent*, or of *Ingleborough*, whilst not lacking altogether the excite-

M

ment of mountain climbing, will introduce him to many scenes of novel character and of astonishing beauty. It is only fair to mention that the Yorkshire waterfalls are second to few in the kingdom.

It is necessary to add a word or two with regard to the coast. The rapidly wasting cliffs to the south of Flamborough are too insignificant for further notice. Flamborough Head, where the chalk attains to a height of 436 ft., is noticed elsewhere. (See *Chalk*.) The line of coast from Flamborough to Saltburn, passing Filey, Scarborough, and Whitby, presents an almost unbroken stretch of cliff, which, however, will find greater favour with the landscape-lover than the climber. These cliffs, which consist chiefly of the oolite and lias series, are throughout crumbling and insecure, and are very frequently composed of little more than clay and shale. *Rockcliff*, or *Boulby Cliff*, however, near Staithes, merits a certain amount of attention. In addition to not a little boldness of outline, it enjoys—or, at any rate, enjoyed —the reputation of being the highest cliff (660 ft.) on the English coast.

PRINTED BY
SPOTTISWOODE AND CO., NEW-STREET SQUARE
LONDON

THE BADMINTON LIBRARY.

Edited by the DUKE OF BEAUFORT, K.G. and A. E. T. WATSON.

ATHLETICS AND FOOTBALL. By MONTAGUE SHEARMAN. With an Introduction by Sir RICHARD WEBSTER, Q.C. M.P. With 51 Illustrations. Crown 8vo. 10s. 6d.

BIG GAME SHOOTING. By CLIVE PHILLIPPS-WOLLEY. With Contributions by Sir SAMUEL W. BAKER, W. C. OSWELL, F. J. JACKSON, WARBURTON PIKE, F. C. SELOUS, Lieut.-Col. R. HEBER PERCY, ARNOLD PIKE, Major ALGERNON C. HEBER PERCY, W. A. BAILLIE-GROHMAN, &c.

Vol. I. Africa and America. With 20 Plates and 57 Illustrations in the Text. Crown 8vo. 10s. 6d.

Vol. II. Europe, Asia, and the Arctic Regions. With 17 Plates and 56 Illustrations in the Text. Crown 8vo. 10s. 6d.

BOATING. By W. B. WOODGATE. With an Introduction by the Rev. EDMOND WARRE, D.D. and a Chapter on 'Rowing at Eton' by R. HARVEY MASON. With 49 Illustrations. Crown 8vo. 10s. 6d.

COURSING AND FALCONRY. By HARDING COX and the Hon. GERALD LASCELLES. With 76 Illustrations. Cr. 8vo. 10s 6d.

CRICKET. By A. G. STEEL and the Hon. R. H. LYTTELTON. With Contributions by ANDREW LANG, R. A. H. MITCHELL, W. G. GRACE, and F. GALE. With 64 Illustrations. Crown 8vo. 10s. 6d.

CYCLING. By VISCOUNT BURY, K.C.M.G. (the Earl of Albemarle), and G. LACY HILLIER. With 89 Illustrations. Crown 8vo. 10s. 6d.

DRIVING. By His Grace the DUKE OF BEAUFORT, K.G. With 65 Illustrations. Crown 8vo. 10s. 6d.

FENCING, BOXING, and WRESTLING. By WALTER H. POLLOCK, F. C. GROVE, C. PREVOST, E. B. MITCHELL, and WALTER ARMSTRONG. With 42 Illustrations. Crown 8vo. 10s. 6d.

FISHING. By H. CHOLMONDELEY-PENNELL. With Contributions by the MARQUIS OF EXETER, HENRY R. FRANCIS, Major JOHN P. TRAHERNE, FREDERIC M. HALFORD, G. CHRISTOPHER DAVIES, R. B. MARSTON, &c.

Vol. I. Salmon and Trout. With 158 Illustrations. Crown 8vo. 10s. 6d.
Vol. II. Pike and other Coarse Fish. With 133 Illustrations. Crown 8vo. 10s. 6d.

GOLF. By HORACE G. HUTCHINSON, the Right Hon. A. J. BALFOUR, M.P. Sir WALTER G. SIMPSON, Bart. LORD WELLWOOD, H. S. C. EVERARD, ANDREW LANG, and other Writers. With 89 Illustrations. Crown 8vo. 10s. 6d.

[OVER.

London: LONGMANS, GREEN, & CO.

THE BADMINTON LIBRARY.

Edited by the DUKE OF BEAUFORT, K.G. and A. E. T. WATSON.

HUNTING. By the DUKE OF BEAUFORT, K.G. and MOWBRAY MORRIS. With Contributions by the EARL OF SUFFOLK AND BERKSHIRE, Rev. E. W. L. DAVIES, DIGBY COLLINS, Sir MARTEINE LLOYD, GEORGE H. LONGMAN, J. C. GIBBONS, and ALFRED E. T. WATSON. With 60 Illustrations. Crown 8vo. 10s. 6d.

MOUNTAINEERING. By C. T. DENT, with Contributions by W. M. CONWAY, D. W. FRESHFIELD, C. E. MATHEWS, C. PILKINGTON, Sir F. POLLOCK, H. G. WILLINK, and an Introduction by Mr. JUSTICE WILLS. With 108 Illustrations. Crown 8vo. 10s. 6d.

RACING AND STEEPLE-CHASING. *Racing*: By the EARL OF SUFFOLK AND BERKSHIRE and W. G. CRAVEN. With a Contribution by the Hon. F. LAWLEY. *Steeple-chasing*: By ARTHUR COVENTRY and ALFRED E. T. WATSON. With 58 Illustrations. Crown 8vo. 10s. 6d.

RIDING AND POLO. By Captain ROBERT WEIR, Riding Master, R.H.G. and J. MORAY BROWN. With Contributions by the DUKE OF BEAUFORT, the EARL OF SUFFOLK AND BERKSHIRE, the EARL OF ONSLOW, E. L. ANDERSON, and ALFRED E. T. WATSON. With 59 Illustrations. Crown 8vo. 10s. 6d.

SHOOTING. By LORD WALSINGHAM and Sir RALPH PAYNE-GALLWEY, Bart. With Contributions by LORD LOVAT, LORD CHARLES LENNOX KERR, the Hon. G. LASCELLES, and A. J. STUART-WORTLEY.

Vol. I. Field and Covert. With 105 Illustrations. Crown 8vo. 10s. 6d.
Vol. II. Moor and Marsh. With 65 Illustrations. Crown 8vo. 10s. 6d.

SKATING, CURLING, TOBOGGANING, and other ICE SPORTS. By J. M. HEATHCOTE, C. G. TEBBUTT, T. MAXWELL WITHAM, the Rev. JOHN KERR, ORMOND HAKE, and HENRY A. BUCK. With 284 Illustrations. Crown 8vo. 10s. 6d.

SWIMMING. By ARCHIBALD SINCLAIR and WILLIAM HENRY, Hon. Secs. of the Life-Saving Society. With 119 Illustrations. Crown 8vo. 10s. 6d.

TENNIS, LAWN TENNIS, RACKETS, and FIVES. By J. M. and C. G. HEATHCOTE, E. O. PLEYDELL-BOUVERIE, and A. C. AINGER. With Contributions by the Hon. A. LYTTELTON, W. C. MARSHALL, Miss L. DODD, H. W. W. WILBERFORCE, H. F. LAWFORD, &c. With 79 Illustrations. Crown 8vo. 10s. 6d.

YACHTING. By Sir EDWARD SULLIVAN, LORD BRASSEY, R. T. PRITCHETT, the EARL OF ONSLOW, LEWIS HERRESHOFF, &c. With 309 Illustrations. 2 vols. Crown 8vo. 10s. 6d. each.

London : LONGMANS, GREEN, & CO.

CPSIA information can be obtained
at www.ICGtesting.com
Printed in the USA
BVOW04s0108050917
493927BV00013BA/127/P